Felinestein

Felinestein

Pampering the Genius in Your Cat

SUZANNE DELZIO and **CINDY RIBARICH, DVM**

Illustrations by Sophia Varcados

HarperPerennial

A Division of HarperCollins*Publishers*

We dedicate this book to those exceptional cat owners
who make a daily effort to provide stimulation
and adventure for their favorite feline friends.

HarperCollins books may be purchased for educational, business, or sales promotional use. For information please write: Special Markets Department, HarperCollins Publishers, Inc., 10 East 53rd Street, New York, NY 10022.

FIRST EDITION

Designed by Helene Wald Berinsky

Library of Congress Cataloging-in-Publication Data

Delzio, Suzanne, 1964–
    Felinestein : pampering the genius in your cat / Suzanne Delzio
and Cindy Ribarich.
        p. cm.
    ISBN 0–06–273630–2
    1. Cats—Training. 2. Cats—Psychology. 3. Animal intelligence.
4. Games for cats. I. Ribarich, Cindy. II. Title.
    SF446.6.D45 1999
    636.8'088'7—dc21   98–43767

01 02 03 04 ❖/HC   8 7 6 5 4 3 2

CONTENTS

ACKNOWLEDGMENTS

First we would like to thank Lisa Ross of the Joseph Spieler Agency and Patricia Medved, who encouraged us to undertake this project. Mary Girard of the Kansas State University College of Veterinary Medicine proved invaluable in our research. We appreciate her efforts greatly. Finally, we'd like to thank all the cat-loving neighbors and friends who gave us insights into the minds of their brilliant pets and allowed us to teach, observe, and challenge their cats in our efforts to accurately devise the tests, activities, and games herein.

PREFACE

Cats. Easy. Low maintenance. No hassle. Give them a house to roam and two meals a day and they're satisfied. That seems to be the conventional wisdom, but those of us in a cat-occupied household know our pets need more.

In our cats' eyes, we're certain we see curiosity, intensity. We wonder what they understand and how smart they are. With all the time they spend alone and unoccupied, we wonder whether they're bored. Most likely, they are.

Veterinary behaviorist Dr. Nicholas Dodman in his recent book, *The Cat Who Cried for Help*, has been the first to raise the alarm that many indoor cats today endure a strange kind of stress: boredom and loneliness resulting from isolation and lack of challenge. Having no responsibilities and nothing against which to match their wits distresses cats, whose minds are still somewhat wired for hard work and tough living. Although we've been domesticating cats for three to four thousand years, our little pets still have many of the same abilities as their scrapping wild cousins. The average free-ranging domestic cat utilizes a territory measuring around one acre. They scramble for meals, constantly honing hunting skills. With survival so tenuous, they fight to protect their dominion from others of their species looking to extend property lines. Wild cats must use their wits daily. While our domestic cats still have these abilities to some extent, they get few opportunities to exercise them. It's this paradox that causes the cat so much stress.

Sometimes cats try to get things going in their environment. They can be a great nuisance, walking across our computer key#%@boards (whoops, there goes one), tossing themselves on their sides directly in our paths. They pester us to get some action starting, to liven the place up a bit. Often owners are too busy or tired to think up ways to entertain them. That's why we wrote this book. Our motivation has much more to do with enriching cats' lives than measuring median feline IQ. Here, we provide cat lovers with more than a hundred practical ways to challenge and amuse their restless wards.

The effort you invest will reward you. Researchers have proven conclusively that you can make your cat (and yourself) smarter. A little challenge, a lot of variety and you're on your way to beefing up his brainpower. He can develop into a better problem solver, a more effective communicator, and a faster learner. Most importantly, you can give him the means to employ his mind and skills.

The intelligence test helps you explore your cat's potential. How great a problem solver is he? Does he have a memory like a trap or do the images flit in and out like the birds in his backyard? Before you know it, the intelligence measurement is over. The remaining six chapters discuss how to provide all sorts of cats with the stimulation to get them exploring, thinking, and making decisions. In these seven chapters, we've included a wide variety of challenges, some for every type of owner and every personality of cat. Incorporating just a few into your cat's life will spark his brainpower and enrich his life.

In a few places, we do assume that cats share a trait or two with humans. We go so far as to use personal pronouns (alternating "he" or "she" from one chapter to the next) rather than the impersonal, icy "it." We believe the assumption that a cat shares no qualities with us is just as misleading. Assuming they don't, however, can be just as misleading. While we don't pretend to know exactly what goes on in a cat's mind, our attitude is: if a little good-natured anthropomorphism helps us bring more fun and adventure into our cats' day-to-day existence, so much the better.

1

Measuring Your Cat's Intelligence

Oh, Me! Call on Me!

$$5 + 3(x-2) = \frac{4}{100}$$
$$\div y^2 (42 + 300)$$
$$\frac{(x-100)}{5+11} + 3$$
$$=$$

Your three pounds of brain matter easily dwarfs your cat's one-ounce thinking machine. Yet, a tiny meow, a few cute prances, and your cat has gotten your work-weary body to rise from the couch and spoon a bit of ice cream into her dish. You swore you weren't going to get up, but you've lost the battle. . . again. No two-legged mammal has ever manipulated you so well.

And how has she done it? Your cat has been observing you, taking notes, drawing conclusions. She's inventoried your soft spots and uses them to bat you around like a catnip mouse. This ability to manipulate testifies to the complexity of your cat's intelligence.

Cat intelligence? How intelligent can a creature with such a tiny head be? What form does her own brand of intelligence take? These tricky questions have perplexed philosophers and scientists for ages. Charles Darwin, our most brilliant observer of the natural world, believed that the difference between human and animal intelligence was one of *degree* rather than *kind*. In other words, Darwin and others held that cats carry out some form of the intellectual functionings that we do.

But there are those dark souls lurking among us who believe differently. Some feel that a cat's mind is so limited, it can't reason, remember past events, or anticipate the future. They also slight our svelte friends for not having language. Without language, the thinking goes, a cat cannot store her experiences and use them to help her make future decisions. These deficits keep cats only in the present moment, acting and reacting from instinct.

We, the authors, are with Charles Darwin and the other enlightened scientists who hold that the cat's mind churns with plans, memories, imaginings, goals, ideas, and emotions. While we may be a bit in the dark as to the extent of these functions, we're confident that the majority of evidence supports our side.

How can we be so sure? Let's skip owners' sweet stories for now and go straight to science. A cat's brain and our brain are made up of the same materials. Not only do they have a cerebrum, a cerebellum, a corpus callo-

sum, a hypothalamus, and a pituitary gland, but their brains utilize the same neurotransmitters we do. Serotonin, epinephrine, and oxytocin cause those pesky feelings such as love, gratitude, appreciation, and shame. In fact, in their book *When Elephants Weep*, Michael Mousaieff Masson and Susan McCarthy make a strong case that because of these structural similarities, animals must experience the same vague phenomenon of emotion we do—at least to some extent.

Likewise, if the structure and substances of a cat's brain come so close to ours, it's not unreasonable to believe that their thoughts—the product of that structure and substance—could be similar, too.

Beyond the basic science, cat behavior suggests that cats do imagine, remember, and reason. Let's start with the fun one: imagination. Part of the scientific community believes that cats, like other animals, react only instinctively to stimuli as they present themselves. The theory goes that cats do not have the imagination to recall previous events or scheme to bring about future ones. Remembering or planning would require the ability to conjure an image that is not currently present, and that far-reaching feat is beyond the cat's abilities. According to this school of thought, imagination and abstract thinking belong to humans alone.

But we've seen plenty of cat memories and plans play themselves out in our homes. We know that a cat can remember the activities she has enjoyed and then prompt us to re-create those conditions. For instance, by swatting a toy toward you, your cat indicates she wants to play. Her desire arises from past play experiences, which she has envisioned and wants to duplicate. Some cats even push their food or water bowls toward their owners, while still others scratch the empty container or even drop toys into it, all in an effort to get food from us. These attempts at communication reveal not only that the cat can imagine what she wants to be doing in the next few minutes, but also that she can associate an object with an activity. Clearly, imagination and abstract thinking help her communicate. She's not stuck in the present, wholly dependent upon instinct. Her previous days impact her present ones. She imagines, and from the insistence with which she voices her demands, her imagination must be quite vivid.

If cats have no memory, how do we explain their change in mood when conditions that previously caused them distress arise again. Does your cat like the carrier that transports her from place to place? Many cat experts stress that you must sneak the cat into the carrier. Why? After being enclosed in it once, she will hate that piece of molded plastic for the rest of her days. It has burned itself into her memory. Cats also develop aversions to people who have treated them badly, without hating the whole human race. Clearly, cats can remember, and they use those memories to make current decisions.

While a good memory characterizes any Einstein, most geniuses report they owe most of their accomplishments to an insatiable curiosity. Cats, too, have been known to poke their noses into all sorts of situations, both safe and dangerous. Frank Hunsicker, an engineer in Fairfax County, Virginia, often loses his cuff links, coins, and pens because of his cat's inquisitiveness. When

these items sit on a dresser, the cat cannot stop herself from leaping to them and knocking them to the floor, one by one. As they fall, she watches each closely, waiting until it lands before swatting another from the dresser. While Hunsicker would like to think his cat is studying the effects of gravity, he believes she's probably just interested in how the object will hit the floor. Curiosity leads both people and cats to greater knowledge and understanding.

What other actions give us a peak into a cat's mind? A keen observer, she learns from the actions of those around her. In fact, she earned the kitty equivalent of a college education from her clever mom. Now, she's learning from you. How long did it take her to master opening the cabinet in which her food is stored after watching you do it? It's usually doesn't take two times.

In fact, smart cats know that watching another is the easiest way to pick up a new skill. At the Brain Research Laboratory at the City University of New York, researchers needed to speed up the time it took to teach their experimental cats new tasks. Grants and research money are tough to come by, after all. Looking for a shortcut, they trained one group of cats to perform a certain task. Then they allowed novice, unexposed cats to watch proficient cats carry out the task. A third group of cats remained unexposed to the task at all times. When challenged with the same task, the novice observer cats performed it well and quickly. The group of cats who didn't have the opportunity to observe trained cats took much longer to figure out the new task. With no previous exposure, they had to learn by doing. Impressed, the researchers concluded that "learning by observation in adult cats is a more efficient method of learning than conventional shaping procedures" (e.g., trial and error). Don't underestimate the cat who spends a lot of time merely watching you. One day you may wake up to find her finishing your taxes.

Sophia Varcados, the book's illustrator, lived with a cat named Orange who was a fast learner. When Sophia talked on the phone, she became somewhat unavailable. Frustrated, Orange quickly learned that if she walked on the cradle of the phone and stepped on the little button there, she would immediately get Sophia's direct attention because the call would end. That Sophia was cross was beside the point. The cat had a goal, and she accomplished it. Whenever Orange was in the room and the phone rang, Sophia (also a fast learner) resorted to covering the button to avoid being instantly disconnected.

Now, the big question: Can cats reason? Can they gather information and draw conclusions based on facts? Seeing that packed suitcase and Hawaii brochure on your bed, your cat throws a tantrum rivaling that of a human toddler. She whines for your attention or, angry, sits a few feet away, her back to you, tail swishing. She knows something's up, and she's not happy about it. After all, she has seen this before. The conditions in the environment tell her that she will be abandoned again. Any *reasonable* cat would conclude the same. Rational thinking enables her to understand the depth of your betrayal.

Granted, on some days your cat may seem a little clueless. Some cats have

been made fools of by clever screen doors that suck in all eighteen of their claws and refuse to let go. Cats have also been known to stalk a visitor's purse or shoes as if these innocent leather items crawled out from the fiery underworld. But then again, Dan Quayle couldn't spell potato, and Richard Nixon tape-recorded his own felonies for all of posterity. We humans have had our famous failings as well.

Imagination, memory, ability to learn by observation, and reason make up the elements of our traditional definition of intelligence. Cats exhibit them all. Because of these similarities, we feel justified in measuring some of the same aspects of intelligence that are measured in many human IQ tests: learning ability, communicative ability, problem-solving ability, and memory. The twenty-four questions in this IQ test help you gauge just where on the intellectual bell curve your cat resides.

Note, however, that only this first chapter deals with measuring your pet's intelligence; the other six chapters cover how to *excite* it. We feel most passionate about this aspect of our book. Yes, we have an agenda. For too long, pet owners have focused only on the physical needs of their cats. This book addresses their intellectual and emotional requirements. Once given a simple program of stimulation and interaction, your cat enjoys her life much more. In fact, many strange, problematic behaviors may abate once the cat begins playing a few games and exploring more corners of the house. More importantly, with enhanced interaction, your relationship with your cat deepens.

The chapters ahead contain activities and environmental modifications to keep your cat's mind churning. A fresh game, a new skill and an exciting environment all help deliver the challenge our domestic cats are missing today. If your cat seems a little slow now, read on. We'll explore what the latest brain research has concluded: You can make your cat (and yourself) smarter.

The IQ Test

Before you start, keep a few things in mind. Getting an accurate measure of your cat's intelligence will depend on clearing up a few issues first. While we hold that there is a range of intelligence in cats that makes some smarter than others, a few obstacles make measuring it difficult. The big issue with cats is motivation. How do we get them to perform the simplest things for us? Most of the Hollywood cat trainers use food. If the cat doesn't respond to food, they find another cat. Some effective kitty treats include a taste of gourmet canned cat food and tartar-control kibble. Try out several to determine which makes her salivate the most. If food doesn't do the trick, your cat may be motivated by toys. Her reward may simply be a sniff of or a look at the new toy you've enticed her with.

When trying to get your cat to work for you, there's also your relationship to consider. Does your cat enjoy being with you, or do you two just tolerate each other? Have you been making an effort to groom or play with her over the years? Does she solicit your attention? Do the two of you understand each other's signals clearly? Do you remember her name? If you have a good relationship, you know when she wants to play, and she knows the right time to jump into your lap for a cuddle.

You know, I just never did well on standardized texts!

If you feel your relationship with your kitty has been neglected for a while, consider skipping the intelligence test for now. Go to Chapter Four: Games and Toys to Keep the Mind Purring, and engage her in some of the fun activities listed there. Using gentle methods, try to teach her one of the tricks we suggest in Chapter Five: Trick Training to Increase Brainpower. After you've worked with her a bit, then attempt the intelligence test. The more learning your cat has had, the better the chances that her score will reflect her true intelligence.

Fatigue and distractions are also score squashers. A tired or irritated brain, human or feline, cannot succeed. Try these tests at a time in the day when your cat is most interested in you. Cats respond well in the morning or when you come home from work. Consider testing before her meal so that her hunger motivates her to get the treat. Test in a familiar area where no loud noises or unexpected events will interrupt. The more ideal the conditions, the better chance the brain has to flex its dendrites to the max.

Researchers have found that the cat will choose the option that requires the least amount of work (big surprise). Therefore, we've done our best to design questions that have equivalent options.

If your cat is sufficiently food-motivated and if the two of you enjoy a strong relationship, there is still her personality to consider. The timid cat often cannot let her true potential shine through. She may be afraid of the equipment or of the unusual requests. Even if you can't measure her IQ, use the rest of the book to enrich her environment and multiply her daily activities. Shy cats have many endearing traits, so if you're frustrated with her score, have confidence that you still have a valuable pet. While she may never be able to score off the charts on an IQ test, she still adds much to your life.

These exercises measure four components traditionally considered part of intelligence:

1. Learning ability—how quickly can your cat retain and then use new information?
2. Problem-solving ability—when faced with an obstacle, how adept is she at surmounting the problem to win the reward?
3. Memory—how long do objects she has seen or tricks she has learned stay in her mind?
4. Communicative ability—how easily does she comprehend your gestures and even your words? How well does she express her desires and manipulate you?

Many of these exercises have humorous choices that are obviously intended to be ignored in scoring. The questions are in random order so that A is not necessarily the best or worst answer. You'll find the scoring key on page 28.

Because many of these questions are somewhat involved, don't expect to complete the test within days or even a week. Your cat will get confused if bombarded with too many new requests at once. Use them as something to do with your furry friend from time to time. Jot down each score as you complete the exercise. At the end of a month, you'll have gathered the information you need to compute her final score.

Because of the limitations inherent in measuring feline intelligence, we encourage you to view the test as an opportunity to get to know your cat's personality and potential—and a chance to strengthen your relationship with her. That the test will help you decide which tier of college applications to send for is only an added bonus.

IQ Test

Learning Ability

1. By now, your cat most likely knows where her food is kept. When she wants it, she rubs or walks in small circles around the cabinet. One day, change its location. Put the food in a different cabinet or, if you want to really test her, a different room. For accuracy, put it in a sealed container so that she can't smell it as well. At dinnertime, call her to the new location. Open the cabinet and show her the food, but put the food bowl in her usual place. If she doesn't go to the new location the next feeding time, show her again. How many times does it take her to start circling and meowing around the new area on her own initiative?

    A. She knew after the first time I showed her.
    B. Two to three times.
    C. More than five times.
    D. After tireless picking at every cabinet door, she finally found it a week later.

2. A cat's learning ability can be measured in part by her accuracy in reading her owner's moods. When you're upset or angry, your cat:
    A. Hides herself away.
    B. Tries to comfort you by rubbing against you, crying, or climbing onto your lap.
    C. Continues to lazily groom herself, lie close by, or sleep.
    D. Dials your pharmacist for your Prozac refill.

3. Cats have an uncanny sense of time. One of the things a cat learns about you is the time of day you carry out certain functions in your life. Cats are

often more reliable than alarm clocks. How well has your cat learned your schedule? Does she know when you get up in the morning?

When it's around your usual rising time, does your cat try to "help" you up by pawing your nose. Cats kept in other rooms during the night accomplish the same thing by pulling at the bottom of the door in the morning, making a lot of noise. Your cat:

A. Wakes you up when she wants to get up; any and all times are fair game.

B. Lies on your face promptly at *her* rising time: 5:30 A.M. A little asphyxia awakens the soundest sleeper.

C. Alerts you to your usual waking time every morning.

D. Remains asleep until you rouse her or keeps herself occupied without disturbing you.

4. Many studies have indicated that cats are capable of "observational learning." The cat who has the opportunity to watch another cat learn something new before she's asked to perform the same task completes that task much more quickly. The cat who doesn't get to observe but must muddle through it by herself takes longer to learn.

For this task, you need a small food bowl and an index card. Make sure the bowl has a wide flat bottom so that the cat doesn't tip it over. Put food in your cat's bowl and cover it with an index card. Make sure one side of the index card is hanging farther over the edge than the other, making it easy to remove. With her watching you, press down on the edge of the index card, flipping it up and off of the food. Allow her to eat. Repeat this process for several days. Encourage the cat and stand back. How many days does it take until she knows to paw at the card?

    A. A week.
    B. Two to three days of me showing her.
    C. She does it the first day I let her.
    D. Never—she turns to my household plants as her dominant food source.

5. Teach your cat to ring a bell. Buy a simple bell or wind chimes at a pet or discount store and hang it from a table or desk. Swing it for your cat, getting her interest. She will naturally paw at it, after she has explored it to make sure it's safe. When she paws at it, making noise, say "ring." By affixing a command to an action a cat is already carrying out, you make training easy. Every time she rings it, say "ring" and give her a special treat. She'll soon learn she can ring to get a treat. You can even help your cat by sitting her in front of the chimes and pushing them with her paw while saying "ring." Don't worry—you're not creating a monster. You can always take down the bells if she becomes a bell-ringing psychopath. How many times do you have to show your cat how to ring the bell before she starts ringing it herself?

- A. Two to three times.
- B. About five times.
- C. More than ten times.
- D. Never—seizing an opportunity, she pulls the bell down and ties it around the dog's neck.

6. Cats learn just as efficiently with a negative stimulus (e.g., a loud "NO" or a stream of water from a spray bottle) as with a positive one (e.g., a treat reward). If you've been wanting your cat to stay off of a piece of furniture or the counter, you can test her intelligence while you train her. Many veterinary clinics and pet stores sell the Snappy Trainer, a spring-loaded cardboard contraption that flips when touched, scaring the cat and hopefully training her to stay away. You can also use pie tins, aluminum foil, double-faced sticky tape, or empty soda cans to serve the same purpose.

Place the Snappy Trainer (or pie tin, soda can, or whatever) on the furniture or counter. How quickly does she learn not to jump there?

A. After the first encounter, she doesn't emerge from under the couch again.
B. After I've found the device moved or tripped two or three times.
C. After I've found the device moved or tripped five to seven times.
D. Bent on revenge, she moved the device to my bed.

Memory

7. To test feline memory, researchers at Pennsylvania State University enticed cats to learn to distinguish between two distinct shapes. Their materials included two bowls, two index cards, and food. With a dark marker, researchers drew an X on one index card and an O on the other. They placed food in one bowl, covering it with the X card. The O card was placed over the empty bowl. So that both bowls smelled of food, they rubbed some food around the empty bowl and then removed it. Despite these tactics, the cats quickly learned to go to the bowl with the X card on top.

You can carry out the same experiment at home. To really motivate the cat, you may want to use your special gourmet cat food for this test. Rub some food on the bottom of one bowl, but make sure to remove it all. Put the cat's usual amount of food in the other bowl. At feeding time, put the two bowls and cards out. Decide which shape or letter will always cover the food. Let the cat explore. At first, you may have to help her get the cards off the top of the bowl. Make sure to switch the bowls' position every day, having the X bowl on the right one day and on the left the next. You want to guarantee that the cat recognizes the letter, not simply the position of the bowl. How many days or trials does it take before the cat goes automatically to the shape that covers the food?

A. Two to three.
B. Around five.
C. Seven to ten.
D. Frightened, I gave up after finding a mysterious card with a strange symbol over my frozen dinner.

8. Plan to put your cat outside of a room she commonly traverses for a day. Once she's outside, rearrange the furniture to some extent. If you don't feel like pushing your couches around, you can put an open umbrella or large box in the middle of the floor. Leave the room for a while and then return to it, leaving the door open so that the cat can join you. When you're in the room, do something you normally do: Watch television, work, or read. Try not to stare at the cat too intently. When your cat comes to join you, she:

A. Seems oblivious to the change.

B. Acts immediately alerted, wandering about the room exploring, either tentatively or aggressively.

C. Hides in terror.

D. Begins exploring the room or object after five minutes or so.

9. Smart cats remember who's good to them and who isn't. Can your cat distinguish between those visitors who have shown her attention and those who haven't? (Note: This question may not apply to the cat who loves everyone with a pulse.)

A. A fair-minded feline, she ignores everyone.

B. She's more affectionate and attention-seeking toward those who've called her name and pet her before.

C. A sadist, she pays most attention to those who hate her, fear her, or are allergic to her.

D. She hides under the bed only to reappear after the last guest leaves.

10. At your cat's regular feeding time, fill her bowl and then put it in a room or corner that you never put it in. Lead the cat to the area, but don't let her get the food. Carry her away from both this area and her usual eating area. Keep her occupied in another room for five minutes. Take her to the area where her food is usually kept and release her. Your cat:

A. Runs past her usual feeding area straight to the new spot you showed her.

B. Stops at her usual area, looking for her dinner, begging for food. She has completely forgotten you've moved it.

C. Stops briefly at her usual area and then runs straight to the new location.

D. Runs helter-skelter around the yard/house looking for her food. She finds it only after a lot of time and effort.

11. Buy a few new toys for your cat. Let her play with them for a week or two until it's obvious that she's bored with them. Put them away for two days. The smart cat remembers the toy over that short of a period and will remain uninterested when it reemerges. (Owners who retire toys to make them seem new again usually put the toys away for two weeks at least.) When you bring the toy out after only two days, your cat:

A. Examines and plays with it for a few moments before walking away from it.

B. Looks at it and yawns before stretching out on your newspaper.

C. Pounces on it like it was brand-new.

D. Swishes her tail, miffed that you have nothing better to offer.

12. Object permanence refers to any animal or person's ability to realize that an object still exists even when she can no longer see or smell it. Kittens don't realize a hidden object still exists until they're 16 weeks old. For these little ones, when a toy or treat can no longer be seen or smelled, it's gone. Maturation solves this problem. Yet, sometimes a cat who has had a very limited environment as a kitten does not develop the necessary neural connections to establish object permanence. This deficit will hinder her response to life's challenges.

To gauge your cat's ability to understand that hidden objects still exist, show the cat a new toy. She will be very curious to inspect it. Once you're sure she's interested, restrain the cat and put the toy under a towel on the floor. It's okay if she sees you doing this. Release the cat. After the toy has "disappeared," your cat:

A. Looks and even wanders away, seemingly having forgotten the toy exists.
B. Crawls under the towel to join the toy for a nice nap.
C. Goes immediately to the towel and tries to get at the toy, successful or not.
D. Looks around the area for the toy.

Problem-Solving Ability

13. Researchers often test for intelligence by rewarding a cat for choosing one of two options. For instance, they give her a choice of going down a white or a black tunnel or of eating from a square or round bowl. Once the

cat is reliably choosing the rewarded option, they switch the conditions and reward for the other option. They note how long it takes the cat to realize conditions have changed and adjust her behavior appropriately. The faster they can change their behavior, the smarter they are.

Appalling! Completely disorganized in here!

We can reproduce this kind of test at home. If you or your cat doesn't like the idea of being enclosed in a small space for a moment, you may want to skip this question and disqualify it from your test. You need a closet that has two sliding doors that overlap. Turn on the closet light, place the cat in the middle of the closet and close the doors. Leave the cat inside for thirty seconds. Open one side quietly, wide enough only to allow the cat to escape. Quickly step back and stand in the middle of the front of the closet. Call the cat. The cat will quickly learn to choose that side. Repeat this several times. Once she comes out of the door you repeatedly open, change the rules. Put the cat in, shut both doors, and open the door you haven't been using. Again, stand in the middle of the closet and call. Your cat:

A. Rearranges your blouses according to color.

 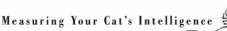

B. Cries and pulls at the door she's accustomed to getting out of.

C. Spends a little time at the door she's used to getting out of and then walks to the open door.

D. Runs right through the open door (correct choice) without even going to the other door.

14. At feeding time, put your cat's favorite treat on a piece of cardboard. To the cardboard, attach a cord or string that's at least three feet long. Find a doorway in your home and put a baby gate in it at about two inches up from the floor. Put the cardboard with the food on the other side of the baby gate, but run the string under the baby gate. Sit on the other side with your cat. Let her watch you pull at the string and pull the food toward you. Repeat this observation experience for a few days. Do not let the cat leap over the gate to get the food. When you think she's ready, encourage her to pull at the string. You can even put her paw on it, thereby pulling the string and panel toward you to help her. When she's ready to go it alone, your cat:

A. Pulls at the string right away, bringing the panel closer to her.

B. Wanders away or seems disinterested, even if hungry.

C. Runs up to the gate and/or jumps over it.

D. Makes any attempt to pull at the string, successful or not.

15. Buy a new toy for your cat and let her play with it for only a few seconds. If she's not turned on by toys, you may as well resort to food again. This has to be something she's truly motivated by. It could be a catnip toy if she likes those. Line up three paper cups in a row. Put the toy under one of them. Holding her, lift the cup and show her the toy. Put the cup back over the toy. Once you let the cat go, she:

A. Looks all around the area for the toy, ignoring all cups.
B. Goes right to any cup and explores it—but fails to get the toy out from under it or chooses the wrong cup.
C. Takes a few minutes to knock over the correct cup.
D. Knocks over the correct cup in under a minute.

16. A natural prey object hides several times in its escape from a cat. Imagine a mouse moving through a field full of rocks and grass clumps. The mouse darts from one barrier to another, hoping to lose the cat. The successful cat notes all obstacles and remembers the last location the prey disappeared. To simulate this situation, set up three boxes (or any small barrier) in a line in your living room. Tape fishing line or string to your cat's favorite toy (or a new toy). Have someone else hold the cat about ten feet in front of your line of boxes. Sitting at the end of the line of boxes, pull the string toward you, allowing the object to pass behind each barrier. Don't pull the object past the third barrier. Instead, let it rest behind it. Tell your helper to release the cat. Which does the cat approach first?

A. The first box.
B. The second box.
C. The third box, finding the toy immediately.
D. Her food bowl.

17. Take a favorite piece of food and let your cat see it. Put it far enough under a couch where she cannot reach it with her mouth. What methods does your cat use to get the piece of food?

A. She keeps banging her nose up against the couch without resorting to her paws.
B. At first she uses her nose but quickly resorts to using her paws and nose.
C. She starts using her paws after a few unsuccessful minutes of trying to get to it with her nose.
D. She shreds the couch until she reaches the treat.

18. Leave a decent-size box on the floor, tipped so that the opening is perpendicular to the ground and the cat can walk in without having to jump. Have a bath towel ready. Once she wanders into the box, cover the opening with the bath towel and tuck the end under the box so that it is a little

challenging for the cat to escape. (Note: Not for the claustrophobic cat.) Your cat:

- A. Pathetically cries for you to save her.
- B. Immediately begins pawing the towel to free herself.
- C. Paws the towel after a few moments of irritated silence.
- D. Plays in the box, then paws at the towel when she's had enough.

Communicative Ability

19. When you talk to your cat, how does she indicate that she understands you are trying to communicate? Does she try to communicate in return? Get her attention and talk to her, frequently using her name. She:

I've detailed a list of my wishes.

- A. Looks into your eyes and makes vocalizations, or behaves in a way that indicates she's more alert.
- B. Looks away or even wanders off.
- C. Stares without responding.
- D. Says, "Hey, maybe you should get out more. . . ."

20. How does your cat indicate that she wants to play?

    A. She throws herself down on her side (in cat body language, this can mean "let's play!").
    B. Rolls a toy toward me or brings me a toy.
    C. Meows at me.
    D. Walks in wearing her gym suit.

21. How effective has your cat become at creating signals of communication to which you respond? When your cat meows at you, do you usually know what's wrong? Does she have different meows and behaviors for different goals? One for food, going out, or to play?

    A. My cat doesn't solicit my attention.
    B. She just sits in my way and meows endlessly. I guess what she wants until I get it right.
    C. I always know what she wants because her motions and meows vary. She even uses an intermediary to signify what she wants (e.g., bringing a toy to you when she wants to play).
    D. She meows for a while and then rolls her eyes and writes her wishes in the sand of her litter box.

22. How competent is your cat at connecting a word with one of your actions? We can check this ability by modifying a common cat discipline technique. One way to deter your cat from jumping on counters and fancy furniture is to spray her with a spray bottle. Any time you see her in these places, give her a spray, saying "OFF" each time you do it. If your cat is smart, she'll connect the stream of water with the word. You'll eventually be able to say "OFF" from wherever you are in the house and she'll jump down. The spray bottle itself will have outlived its usefulness. Use the spray bottle with the word for a couple of weeks before you drop the bottle. How quickly does your cat start responding simply to the word "OFF"?

A. One week or less.
B. Two to three weeks.
C. I give up after a month.
D. Never—she begins freezing in place, thinking she'll pass for a knicknack.

23. Come up with a name that sounds similar to your cat's name. When your cat is lounging peacefully, turn toward her and call her using this variation. How does she respond?

A. She turns her head a bit, but I've got to get it exactly right to merit her attention.
B. She becomes as alert and responsive as when I call her by her real name.
C. She doesn't respond at all.
D. She pats your hand and explains that senility can set in at any time.

24. How well does your cat understand your signals and body language? When the two of you are in a room together, look at her until she looks back at you. Slowly, let happiness spread over your face—smile, let your eyebrows rise. How does your cat respond?

A. Frowns and asks, "Have you been sniffing my catnip again?"
B. Her eyes widen, her ears turn toward me, or she narrows her eyes in a "love squint."
C. She rises and approaches me.
D. She looks away, looks past me, or continues to stare blankly.

KEY:

Note which group of exercises your cat was most adept at solving. Like people, cats may be stronger in one area of intelligence than another. One cat will be a great problem solver. Another will be a quick study, learning the new location for the cat food more quickly that your spouse does. Understanding your cat's strengths and weaknesses can help you decide which games and activities she will most enjoy.

1.		2.		3.	
A.	4	A.	4	A.	2
B.	3	B.	4	B.	2
C.	1	C.	0	C.	4
D.	0	D.	0	D.	0

4.	A. 2	9.	A. 0	14.	A. 4
	B. 3		B. 4		B. 0
	C. 4		C. 3		C. 0
	D. 0		D. 0		D. 3
5.	A. 4	10.	A. 4	15.	A. 0
	B. 3		B. 0		B. 3
	C. 2		C. 3		C. 3
	D. 0		D. 2		D. 4
6.	A. 4	11.	A. 3	16.	A. 2
	B. 3		B. 4		B. 3
	C. 3		C. 0		C. 4
	D. 0		D. 4		D. 0
7.	A. 4	12.	A. 0	17.	A. 0
	B. 3		B. 0		B. 4
	C. 2		C. 4		C. 3
	D. 0		D. 2		D. 0
8.	A. 0	13.	A. 0	18.	A. 1
	B. 4		B. 0		B. 4
	C. 4		C. 3		C. 3
	D. 2		D. 4		D. 4

19. A. 4	**21.** A. 0	**23.** A. 4
B. 0	B. 2	B. 1
C. 2	C. 4	C. 4
D. 0	D. 0	D. 0
20. A. 4	**22.** A. 4	**24.** A. 0
B. 4	B. 3	B. 4
C. 3	C. 0	C. 4
D. 0	D. 0	D. 0

SCORE:

Felinestein: 80–96 points
Definitely College Bound: 70–79 points
Average Joe: 60–69 points
Happy-Go-Lucky: 59 points and under

2

Kitten Kindergarten

JUMP-STARTING THE KITTEN'S BRAIN

**Give Me the Yellow!
My Turn
with the Yellow!**

If you got your hands on this book before you picked up your kitten, you're in luck. For all mammals, the brain learns fastest and easiest in the juvenile stage. If you make smart rearing choices while your kitten is still young, you can mold his somewhat disorganized brain into a confident, curious, and powerful tool. While he'll never take the bar exam for you, he may find his lost toys quicker and become more adept at escaping from a tangle of clothes. Your kitten's environment, his relationships, and the challenges he faces now shape his mind and adult personality.

Literally shape his mind? Yes. Unlike the heart or lungs, which are born small but complete, the brain at birth is still in process. In feline (and human) adulthood, billions of individual brain cells (neurons) connect through places called "synapses." But at birth many of these synapses haven't been formed yet. The neurons remain unconnected. Just what patterns they do form is largely determined by environment.

In other words, a creature's genetic code is not the only boss in the brain factory. Experiences also prompt brain cells to reach romantically toward each other, laying down memories and actions similar to the way city planners develop networks of roads to connect different suburbs. The more connections between cells, the more capable and efficient the brain.

Ironically, to accommodate all this growth and change, a mammal's brain emerges with far too many brain cells. By adulthood, both humans and cats retain only about half of the brain cells they were born with. Unused, the other half die off. Neuroscientists agree that during the early part of life the overgrown brain gets a serious trim. Which and how many brain cells remain depends largely on input from the outside world.

Because this shaping must take place early, all mammals learn best when they are immature. For human children, the ideal learning window occurs between four and ten years of age. For cats, it opens between two and seven

weeks. Young brains simply encode learning and experience more efficiently than older brains do.

To take advantage of the brain's Major Sponge Period, researchers have experimented to determine the effect of environment on development. Dr. Marian Diamond, a University of California at Berkeley neurobiologist, has done some fascinating work on how environment can change the physical structure of the brain. In her research, she gave one group of baby rats an "enriched environment," which included exercise devices, lots of opportunity for socialization, and toys that were changed often. Another group of rats was raised in a cage with no toys or exercise devices. She found that baby rats in the enriched environment seemed mentally quicker and more energetic than those who grew up with few or no toys. Further, the enriched rats got through mazes more quickly and faced challenges with less stress.

Since observational evidence can be deceptive and subjective, Diamond looked further. The most fascinating finding came when she examined the rats' brain tissue. There she discovered that the stimulated rats had longer, more extensive nerve cells. The amount of chemicals between the nerve cells (neurotransmitters) of the challenged rats had also increased. The enriched environment helped the brain develop to its maximum potential. With a supercharged brain, it's no wonder these special rats zoomed through mazes and tackled challenges with bravado.

So excited by her results and those of similar studies, Dr. Diamond helped set up a special preschool for disadvantaged children. The school provides the enrichment opportunities these children may not otherwise receive. The ultimate goal is to make sure these children do not remain behind their peers. By jump-starting their students' minds with specialized activities, Diamond and her colleagues have achieved remarkable results.

It's not only rats and kids whose brilliance blooms with exposure to a variety of challenging activities. In similar tests with kittens and puppies, the subjects who were given socialization, enrichment, and early handling had these similarities:

1. Enhanced learning abilities because of emotional stability
2. Outgoing personalities that lead them into learning situations
3. Greater resistance to physical and emotional stress and diseases

These studies demonstrate how a few environmental modifications can make all the difference in the lives of many types of animals. A kitten with an enriched early life is not only smart but also a better pet. First, he's more entertaining. His enhanced interest in toys and new environments makes him fun to watch and play with. Since you've taken steps to direct his energy to appropriate objects and games, a higher percentage of your household heirlooms remain unexplored (in other words, unscratched and unmauled). In addition, a kitten with a high-octane brain responds more quickly to your signals and moods. Your subtle and not so subtle hints do not go over his head but register and are responded to. Finally, the schooled kitty solves problems better (which may or may not be good for you, especially if the "problem" involves a pan of delicious chicken perched high on the counter). Kitten owners reading this book have an ideal chance to create wonderful pets.

The Mother's Influence on Her Kitten's Early Learning

Unfortunately for owners, the cat's ideal learning period takes place before we get a chance to flip our first flash card. Breeders and pet-store owners, along with the kitten's mother and siblings, oversee the kitten's first weeks. In fact, it's best that the kitten stay with its mother and siblings until he's twelve weeks old. Kittens separated from their families early are poorer learners. They also develop emotional and behavioral abnormalities. While we usually can't get our hands on our cats in their first weeks, we should explore the life he had before we took him home.

The mother's influence, the environment, and nutrition all play a part in how bright, curious and well-adjusted a kitty will be. Let's consider the mother first. The first and most effective teacher, Mom models social, maternal, and hunting skills. While instinct also affects these talents, kittens learn the finer points involved by watching the experienced elder they adore. Female kittens with attentive mothers become good mothers themselves. The offspring of adept hunters also hunt better than those kitties that observed their mothers pouncing too early and stalking too close. Mother cats can even teach their kittens which members of the human household to prefer. This influence explains why some cats seem to love men while others prefer women from the start. When choosing a kitten, asking the breeder how well the mother cat cared for and taught her kittens increases the odds that you're taking home a stable, intelligent pet.

It's not only the mother's teaching skills that affect the kitten. Her personality and circumstances shape his intelligence as well. A calm, confident mother encourages a kitten to explore his environment. The more the kitty explores, the more he learns, remembers, and tackles challenges. A nervous or shy mother sends the message to the kitten that the experiences the world offers should be avoided. While owners have taken casual notice of this modeling, researchers gathered concrete facts confirming its influence. Several studies show the offspring of shy mothers responding timidly to a variety of stimuli. In your list of breeder questions, how shy or confident the mother is should not be excluded.

It's smart, too, to go back even further to when the kitten was snug in the womb with his brothers and sisters. During pregnancy, if the mother cat was stressed from lack of food or the presence of aggressive cats, she delivers nervous, emotional kittens. Unable to face challenges and new situations with cool dignity, these nervous kitties can't learn as well as their confident counterparts. Kittens with inadequate nutrition while in the womb crawl, suck, climb, walk, and play more slowly than kittens with a well-fed mother. In addition, the deprived kittens tend to be antisocial. If the food supply continues to be short after the kittens are born, the development of organs (including the brain) can be affected. Kittens undernourished in the womb and during the early weeks of life were slower, suffered more accidents and performed poorly on tests. The mother's circumstances while she carried her kittens affect their delicate intelligence. All of these potential negatives make choosing a kitten more complex than one would initially think.

While the kitten's fetal experience can impact his adult personality, rest assured that most pregnant, domestic cats today enjoy a great deal of pampering from their caretakers, whether these concerned folks are breeders or pet owners. The expectant mom probably has enough food and protection to ensure that the kitties she carries dwell in a peaceful, healthy environment.

While the mother and siblings' influence on your cat is the most important, his human caretaker also impacts his personality and intelligence. Whether the person from whom you acquired the kitten turns out to be your neighbor, a farmer, or a professional breeder, he or she has a great deal of responsibility. If the owner is not a professional breeder, chances are that the kitten grows up tussling and learning mostly with his litter mates. As long as nutrition was adequate, that's fine. A dedicated few even stimulate their kittens with activities that enhance their intelligence. Most professional breeders are dedicated to creating healthy, well-adjusted cats. For a few cat breeders, however, the rewards are strictly financial. No matter the motivations and circumstances of the breeder or owner, it's important to ask your kitten's first owner a few questions.

Here are some tips for bringing home a bright, well-adjusted kitten.

1. Ask about the mother's temperament and circumstances. Is she shy or outgoing? A patient or frazzled caregiver? Was she well-nourished? Where did she come from? Was she a stray or a household pet?

2. Ask about the father's temperament and circumstances. Is he friendly? In an ideal situation, you could interact with both the mother and father to assess their personalities for yourself. This contact is the ultimate reassurance.

3. Find out when and in what ways the breeder started interacting with his kittens. Does the breeder believe in the early handling regimen we suggest below?

4. Determine how the kitten got along with siblings. Ask whether he was the timid one of the lot or a playful explorer. Better yet, if the kitten is still around his siblings, ask for the chance to observe him interacting with them.

5. If you do go to a breeder, find out whether it's a Cat Fanciers of

America certified cattery. Those who bother to get certification must meet the CFA's strict standards.

6. Ask to see the premises where the cats are kept. Check for cleanliness and overcrowding.

7. Ask if you can get a veterinary exam prior to your final commitment to keeping the kitten. If not, be wary.

8. Look into your rights regarding the sale of healthy pets in your state. Regulations vary.

9. Research the breed to determine whether the cat is right for you.

Would you mesh better with a high-energy or a low-energy cat? Some breeds require more care than others. A high-maintenance Persian may exhaust you. Ask about genetic problems common to the breed, and consider whether you're prepared to deal with the bills, time, and energy that may result from them.

If you manage to actually plan the acquisition of (rather than impulse buy) your kitten, this list will help you base your choice on factors greater than cuteness. Those prone to falling in love with the kitty at the pet store or in the neighbor's backyard should simply keep their list with them. When that little pink nose points your way, the list will help you stay rational, even if the kitten is adorable. No matter from whom you acquire your cat, you can get a majority of these questions answered.

Stimulation in the Neonatal Period: 0–2 Weeks

Those of us lucky enough to be involved in our kittens' lives before they even open their eyes can and should do many things to encourage brain growth. The activities below can be accomplished without removing kitty from its mother or threatening their relationship. If you don't have the mother cat and her litter in your home, you can ask the breeder or original owner if he or she made some effort to stimulate her kitties in the first two weeks of life. Impressed with the results, veterinarians and experienced cat lovers embrace this low level of stimulation. It can only help your cat.

To stimulate the neonatal kitten, owners should:

1. Pick it up and stroke it for five minutes every day.
2. Whisper to it in a calm, even tone for a few minutes (cats spoken to in the neonatal phase were more responsive to the human voice).
3. Put the kitten on a variety of surfaces so that he learns textures other than those of the litter box, again for only a few minutes. Any unfamiliar surface—a wool blanket, silk scarf, or hardwood floor—will do.
4. Pass items with moderate smells under his nose. A handful of cat food, a piece of lightly scented tissue, or banana all have odors that won't irritate the kitten.

If you approach gently and have a good relationship with the mother cat, she should have no problem loaning her kittens to you for a few minutes each day. The benefits you and the cat will enjoy are well worth the energy you'll expend.

These simple tasks reap great dividends. Dr. Eileen Karsh, while a professor of psychology at Temple University, studied cat behavior extensively. She and other researchers found that neonatal kittens that were picked up, spoken to, and exposed to a variety of smells and textures for several minutes each day developed larger brains with more connections between nerve cells. As we mentioned before, more neural connections translate into more brainpower. These pampered kitties had other advantages as well. Earlier to emerge from the nest box, they got a jump-start on other littermates when it came to exploring their environment. Used to people and sites outside of the nest box, they approached strange toys and humans more readily. Further, handling and stimulation reduced "emotional reactivity," producing kittens with little fear of new situations. Finally, handled kittens were more physiologically resistant to stress later in life. Those of us responsible for neonatal kittens should take advantage of the incredible ability of the young brain to mold a creature's traits and abilities.

Stimulating the Kitten in the Socialization Period: 3–7 Weeks

During the period between three and seven weeks of life, the kitten starts to form relationships with whatever species it encounters. Cats have been known to befriend birds, goats, and even dogs. The socialization period is short, and humans must make a point to get involved in the kitten's life before it finishes this stage. If introduced to their first human as late as ten weeks, the kitten may never bond to its two-legged, furless cohabitants.

If you don't acquire the cat until after this sensitive period, don't panic. Any human, the breeder or former owner, who introduces himself to the three- to seven-week-old kitty will prepare it for your presence. While humans eventually become more important, remember that in these first two months, the cat still learns best from Mom and siblings. If you are involved with your kitten during the socialization period, you can continue the limited regimen of stimulation you started in the neonatal period. At this time, leave most of the instruction to the rest of the cats.

Sorry, I'm reading. . . .

Come on, chase me!

A kitten matures quickly. By three weeks of age he can distinguish smells and see well enough to find his mother. By four weeks he can hear almost as well as an adult. This is also the time he starts to walk and play with littermates.

With all his senses coming online, a kitten's individual personality begins to emerge. The brawlers distinguish themselves from the sensitive, quiet types.

Personality and energy level become apparent. In his book *Supercat: Creating the Perfect Feline Companion,* veterinarian and behaviorist Dr. Michael Fox suggests owners take steps to guide the cat's personality for his long-term well-being. Since an assertive kitty is generally better adjusted as an adult than a shy kitty, intervening now with the timid kitty will help it in the long run. If you have a timid kitty, Fox advises owners to start playing gently with it using a small toy. Get more assertive as the kitty does. Playing like this will maximize any natural assertiveness he may have. Remember, a brave cat explores and learns more, giving it better coping and cognitive skills.

Similarly, the mellow kitty can be set on a more active course in these early weeks. The energetic cat runs headlong into one exciting experience after another. The low-energy cat misses intellectual enhancement opportunities when it foregoes a trek through the garage for a nice nap on the bed.

Before you try to get your slower cat moving, first make sure that his lower energy level has nothing to do with any health problems. The kitten could be suffering from anemia or cardiac problems. Once you've ruled out any health concerns with the help of your veterinarian, Fox suggests that you try to get the kitty moving. Encourage him to chase objects. You can also pair this sleepy guy with a more active brother or sister. Put the two of them alone in a room with the most fun toys. The slower kitty may have to struggle to keep up with the fun, but you may help him to develop more active habits.

That cat personalities can be quite varied shouldn't surprise you. In many mammalian families, extroverts and introverts exist as brothers and sisters. Leah Long of Emlenton, Pennsylvania, could see the personality differences in her cat's offspring early on. So, too, unfortunately, did the cat, Fluffy. Among Fluffy's five kittens were Sam and Skippy, both males. The moment these two stepped from the nest, they started on their distinct courses through life. Outgoing and active, Sam wasn't much of a cuddler. He played aggressively, assailing new objects and experiences. Skippy, on the other hand, begged for attention from anything with a heartbeat, cats and humans alike. When a new toy was introduced, he cringed near the nest or another kitten while someone else explored it first. It didn't take long for Fluffy to pick her favorite son: Sam. She spent most of her time with Sam, happily grooming and playing with him. She even seemed to curry his favor. Cruelly (and without the guidance of a parenting class), she let Skippy know he was a big disappointment. As Skippy lounged in his favorite chair, without warning, Fluffy would stop what she was doing, stroll over to Skippy and pummel him. Shocked, Skippy always fled, even when he grew larger than his mother. The rest of the time she ignored her gentle son. While Sam was

Fluffy's favorite, Skippy got the adoration he needed from the humans of the household. Though it may baffle us, we can't deny that both conquerors and cuddlers can spring from the same mother and father.

Stimulating the Weaned Kitten: 8 Weeks and Older

At eight weeks to twelve weeks, the kitten arrives in our home and we become surrogate parents. Knowledge helps us be the best parent we can. Before you put the math and puzzle problems under his nose, however, your first job is to cement your relationship with him. The quality of your connection with your cat is much more important than his intellectual prowess (after all, he's never going to grab your briefcase and go to work for you). Building that bond will take consistency, discipline, and effort.

For a long time researchers thought that feeding forged the primary link between a dominant and subordinate species. In other words, cats supposedly bonded to us only because we fed them. In an important study again by Eileen Karsh of Temple University, petting and playing proved to be the factors that best facilitated the bonding process. Specifically, the more playing and petting, the stronger the bond. Based on these findings, Karsh concluded that the most solid relationships between owner and cat occurred when they spent at least forty minutes a day interacting. Many cats demand more. As smart as we are, we haven't yet developed the technology to resist their coy manipulation. Between lap-sitting while watching television and attending us as we preen in the morning, these forty minutes are usually taken up without a thought. Keep in mind that each caress, each moment spent in play or talking, reinforces your connection with your cat, a bond the cat needs for his emotional health.

Kitty's Environment

Now that you understand the opportunity you have to beef up your kitten's brain, here are some specifics about how to do so. Despite the fact that we want the best for our kitties, today's realities make it hard to give him the stimulation he needs. With owners away much of the day, the kitten spends a lot of time alone. Nonetheless, you can provide an enriched environment that will nourish his mind.

Since the first few days in a new environment stresses the kitten, it's wise to acquire him over the weekend so that you'll be there with him the first two days while he acclimates. If you have another cat at home, a two-week quarantine is a must.

Now, where to keep him? A small room with a litter box in the corner works for the first week or two while the kitten struggles to take everything in. After he's used to his new life, however, it's time to open up his horizon. You can't fit exercise equipment or very many toys in a small room. A barren area does nothing to maximize kitty brainpower. With nothing to do or explore, kitty usually sleeps. The limited surroundings keep his experiences limited.

To develop a first-class mind, a kitty needs more in his living quarters than litter. Cats are explorers. Their wild cousins creep through undergrowth, climb trees, bat at bugs on a stream's surface, and have endless adventures. The more escapades kitty can get into, the more his brain's nerve cells stretch toward one another. A cat with many opportunities to make choices becomes alert and quick. Which toy do I play with? Should I climb the cat post or burrow through this box? The decision process fuels the mind. Here are some things you can do to make a Feline Wonderland any cat would relish.

What should we play with first?

- Fill the room with toys (make sure they're large and safe enough that he can't swallow pieces of them). Ten different toys are not too many, and more would be even better. Catalogs such as R.C. Steele Wholesale Pet Supply (800–872–3773) and others carry toys at costs much lower the pet supply and grocery stores. Through the catalogs, you can even get three high-quality toys in a batch for around seven dollars. Remember, kitty toys don't have to be bought in a store. The cap from the milk jug, wads of paper, Ping-Pong balls, a crumpled piece of aluminum foil, the top from a twist-off soda, or a cap from a hairspray bottle can be just as fun to the kitty as something that cost $14.95 at a pet store.

- Rotate groups of toys. Keep the same toys in the kitten's environment for two weeks. Pick them up, wash them, and put them away. Bring out other toys and repeat the process. It would be great if you could have four different groups of toys. Leaving unused toys out diminishes their novelty. It's novelty that keeps those neurotransmitters pumping.

- Make sure the toys are of all varieties. Buy a few fur mice, plastic wheels, and balls with bells. The different textures, noises, and shapes will keep the kitty busy investigating.

- Place platforms of different heights around the kitty's area. A phone book will do, as will a stack of large books. To be extra safe, there are many kitty trees sold in the pet stores that are very stable and easy to climb. Climbing on objects will give him a new perspective and teach him new skills.

- You can also make a great place for exploration by taping together a series of boxes. Cats love exploring dark tunnels and byways. Start with typical big, square boxes and cut two kitty-size holes in the sides. Hook them together with a long cylindrical box. You can get as elaborate as you like, just make sure a kitty can navigate the inner depths easily. You may want to have some small windows for light, and an open door at the entrance so that the kitten doesn't get all turned around in the dark. An escape hatch may be wise as well.

- Make sure to have a nice covered bed for him to retire to. He needs this place to recharge. The more emotionally secure a cat feels, the more likely he is to explore and accept challenges.

- Leave a radio playing in his living area. Not only will the human voices be comforting, but they'll get your kitty accustomed to different words and tones of voice. When you speak to him later, he'll have a stronger frame of reference.

- Start now getting your kitten used to a harness. If he learns to walk on a leash now, he'll be more willing to go for walks with you in the future. He can enjoy the stimulation and fun of taking walks for his entire adult life. Harness training is discussed in Chapter Three.

- Skip to Chapter Five: Trick Training to Increase Brainpower and start training your kitten to do tricks now. Most owners and professionals who have trained their cats to do tricks claim that they are most successful when they start the process in kittenhood.

A planned, stimulating environment will provide plenty of challenges for your kitty's developing brain. These modifications are not too tough to pull off, and they'll make a huge difference not only in the kitten's daily life but also in his personality as an adult. In a study from Pennsylvania State University, kittens exposed to a "playground" like this made 34 percent fewer errors in a maze test than those without the experience. Evidence proves that after your efforts to educate your kitten, you'll be rewarded with a smarter, happier cat.

Owner Comes Home at Last!

Your kitten may have played in his playground all day, but when you return after a long day's work, his energy resurges. These activities will help strengthen your bond and help the kitten grow familiar with human language and the process of learning. When you get home, make a point to:

1. Massage and groom. These activities will help the kitten trust you. A kitten with a consistent, caring owner develops confidence in his own abilities to deal with challenges.

2. To all you overprotective types: Don't jump in and solve all his problems for him! If he gets tangled in the curtains, give him a chance to get himself out. If a toy is stuck under a bureau and he's crying, let him try a few solutions. Don't rush in and wipe the problem away. Permitting him to do these things will give him a sense of confidence and control. Allow him to explore and try different strategies to overcome obstacles, even if it takes longer than if you bounced in and took care of it. Overprotectiveness on our part interferes with his independence. Forbidding autonomy limits intelligence as the kitten turns over all the decisions to you. Of course, if the situation is truly hopeless, step in like a good parent and save the day.

3. Give your kitten opportunity for both social play and object play. As far as object play, a living room full of toys will satisfy his desire to bat small things. Social play involves wrestling with another kitten (or your hand). Object play is more predatory: The kitten stalks and chases an object. The desire for social play peaks at about five weeks while the kitten is still with the litter. The desire for object play peaks at seven weeks. Still, the kitten will engage in both types of play throughout his adult life. Provide means for him to participate in social play by wrestling with him with a stuffed animal. Some brave souls even sheathe their hands with socks, giving the kitten a fun opponent.

   Be careful, however, not to encourage aggressive play—biting and scratching in particular. If the kitty starts getting rough, do not put up with it. Each time a claw or tooth comes into contact with your skin, institute some corrective measures. Veterinary behaviorist Dr. Karen Overall suggests owners startle the cat with a loud "NO" or by blowing a quick puff of air in his face. This interruption must take place as closely as possible to the aggression, ideally no longer than thirty seconds thereafter. Overall also recommends ending the play by putting the cat in a room away from you for a ten-minute time-out. Never retaliate by smacking the kitten. Your aggression may induce the cat to become even more physical. In general, substituting a toy for your hand or toes helps you avoid injury and keeps the game going longer. Redirecting the cat toward a toy and away from your body parts helps prevent him from battering any person who happens to dangle a hand his way.

4. With each activity you engage in with your cat, name it. Saying "time for dinner" or "play with mouse?" encourages him to listen to your voice to get an indication of your actions. Don't make the mistake of thinking that your cat doesn't understand your words.

5. Consider keeping a few toys away from the kitty during the day. When you come home, bring out those four or five to play with him. That way, his play with you is more special. He will be motivated to play even more. Once the evening is over, put them away. These toys will have added value, because they are not available all the time.

6. To address his need for social play, encourage your kitty to chase you. Get his attention, and then run into another room and call him. Once he gets the hang of it, hide from him. Before you know it, he'll start eliciting a chase game from you.

7. Allow him to climb over you. The perfectly flat floor gets dull.

8. Let him paw at as many household objects as you can stand. He wants to change their position to discover an object's dimensions and potential.

9. Once you're home, allow the kitty to explore other areas of the house (if you don't already give him free run of the place). Cats learn by accident. He'll lean against a door and it will open. He'll find an obstacle and learn to climb under or around it. Serendipitous encounters stock his store of knowledge and strengthen his problem-solving skills.

10. Take him to a few places other than your home. Remember, this is the stage when the cat learns how the world is. Teach him that the world is an exciting place to be explored with your guidance. Under your supervision, allow him to socialize with other animals, people, and children.

11. Get him comfortable with some of the things that send a number of adult cats flying under the bed. Play music, varying the sound level. If you can get a recording of a thunderstorm, listen to it with him

while you both play as if no threats are near. Vacuum in a room adjacent to the kitten. Start taking him on short car rides. While participating in these activities, keep a calm, happy demeanor yourself. When stresses arise, animals take a cue from us as to how to respond.

A invigorating environment and meaningful interaction with you will augment many of his cognitive skills. If you're looking specifically to create a feline Sherlock Holmes, these activities help him become a better problem-solver as an adult:

- Put him in a cardboard box with the flaps closed but moveable. Call him and see if he can push open the flap and come to you.

- While playing with him, hide his toy under your hand, a pillow, or a towel. Let him search for it for a while, but also allow him to be successful. Give him hints by lifting the corner of the barrier up so that he can see the toy. This exercise is probably more effective after the kitten is sixteen weeks old, after he develops object permanence.

- Put him at the bottom of two stairs and encourage him to climb them. You'll probably have to sit up the stairs from him and encourage him to come to you.

- Put a favorite toy just inside the flap of a cardboard box so that he can see it but must battle the flaps to get to it.

- Pile up a bunch of old pillows. Put him on one side, then go to the other side and sit down. Call him to you. Allow him to crawl over and navigate the pillows. Don't be surprised if he can't resist the soft cushions calling to him to curl up for a nap.

- Put him in one room and go to an area you don't usually occupy. Call him and let him find you.

Adolescence and Adulthood: After 5 Months

At five months, play naturally begins to die down. That may sound sad, but kitten owners across the globe rejoice once their kitten's mania begins to wane. Cats will play throughout their lives. How often and how vigorously they do so as adults depends on you and their developing personalities. We've mentioned that play keeps cats physically and emotionally healthy as well as intellectually stimulated. Therefore, it's well worth the effort to elicit play from your cat throughout its life. We'll discuss the specifics of playing styles and strategies in depth in Chapter Four: Toys and Games to Keep the Mind Purring.

As the stage of kitty innocence ends, we begin to glimpse what the cat will be as an adult. During your cat's adolescent months, watch out for bold behavior. Your sweet furball may be harboring notions of grandeur in that little head of his. Like dogs, cats can come to see themselves as your superior, your boss. If this happens, he'll feel he has license not only to growl and hiss at you but to avoid any request you make of him. While dominance aggression does not fully emerge in cats until they are between two and four years old, it's wise to institute rules and attitudes now so that you won't have to readjust the power structure later.

To sidestep the troubles that accompany dominance, when you bring your kitten home, set up some household regulations and enforce them consistently. Your assertiveness keeps any grand notions far from the cat's plans. In a world set up and directed by humans, cats need a human to lead. The best cat owner accepts the responsibility he's undertaken and enforces limits to keep his cat safe.

Some good cat rules are:

1. No cats on the counters.
2. Outside cats must come inside at dusk.
3. No begging while humans are eating.
4. No pulling on doors to make them bang.
5. No pleas for affection when you're on the toilet, on the computer, or on the phone. (Even the bravest cat owners usually lose this battle. Those of you who allow your cats on your laps when you're on the toilet, we're onto you!)

If you never set up any household rules before, you may want to take a few days to detect just who directs whom in the household. A cat who believes he is superior to you often:

You don't wanna come in here....

- Bites while being petted
- Hisses or bites when moved from a resting place
- Resists petting
- Stands directly in your path or moves in the way of a piece of furniture you're heading for
- Seeks attention when you're distracted (on the phone, in particular)

If your cat demonstrates several of these behaviors, Dr. Karen Overall recommends taking a tough-love approach that will show him who is the boss.

1. If the cat is on your lap and begins exhibiting signs that he's about to bite or scratch, break the progression immediately. When his ears go flat, he stares menacingly, or his body becomes tense, stand up and

let the cat fall from your lap. It's best to deliver this rude awakening within the first seconds the cat starts demonstrating "attitude."

2. Consider withholding affection from the cat. If he does condescend to sit in your lap, stroke him only a few times, ending the attention when you want to.

3. If the cat is curled in your Lazy Boy keeping you on the floor with a menacing stare, regain your rightful furniture. Do not let the cat tell you where you'll sit or walk. To avoid a more intense battle and possible injury, use a broom handle to move the cat, not your hand.

4. Owners with cats that give little warning of impending aggression can carry a water pistol or foghorn with them whenever they're close to the cat. The minute a claw is raised or a lip curled, let fly with the annoying sound or water stream.

As a preventative measure, training the cat establishes just who takes the orders and who gives the orders in the household. Chapter Five: Trick Training to Increase Brainpower discusses many fun tricks that painlessly convey your supremacy.

In Short...

Oh, how innocent he looked in the store. How fiendish he became once entering your home. He topples the Tupperware. He soars from the couch to

your pant leg, where he hangs desperately. He performs life-threatening headstands in your work boots.

Take heart. Embarked on the most rapid learning period of his life, he's taking in the whole world, exploring his abilities and testing the boundaries of other household members. It will all be over soon. Whether he matures into an interesting, curious cat or a sleepy lump hinges on what kind of environment you provide. The more you give him now when you're home and even when you're not home, the more confident and balanced he'll be. With a few modifications, you can set your kitty up for a stable, stimulating life.

3

Home Alone

THE INDOOR CAT'S GUIDE TO FILLING HER DAYS

*C*lutching your briefcase and coffee, you stumble out of the door to begin your 7 A.M. commute. As the car key crunches into the lock, out of the corner of your eye you see the upstairs curtain tremble. You should rush into the car, but stop to look up. Pawing the curtain aside, kitty presses her pink nose to the window. Her eyelids bat over two forlorn eyes. She opens her mouth, but her meow cannot penetrate the glass. Kitty is alone. And you—you beast—have left her.

Ah, the life of the solitary indoor cat. While bosses yell at us, coworkers annoy us and we struggle to stay ahead of the game, our cats eat and sleep the day away. You'd like a life like that. . . you think. Keep in mind that it's these underchallenged indoor cats that turn up with bizarre behaviors. The absence of variety, activity, and even a moderate level of stress can be as detrimental as too much chaos and uncertainty.

Witnessing the lazy life of the cat, it's tough to believe that she suffers. But chronic boredom and loneliness are unnatural for any mind. The busier the family, the less occupied the cat—and today's families are busier than ever. Pet owners are no longer home for the majority of the day. Alone, our cats don't have the chance to observe tussles between siblings, kitchen accidents and visits from neighbors. When we do come home, we're often too beat to give her the play and petting she deserves. Unlike a dog, when neglected, the cat won't stand on her head to solicit attention (and she looks down on the dog who does). Instead, the cat becomes more and more aloof. That's not good for either of you.

In its worst incarnation, chronic boredom may land you both in the veterinarian's office. As we mentioned in Chapter One: Measuring Your Cat's Intelligence, the last twenty years have seen a surge in cases where cats exhibit serious behavioral problems with no physical cause. Compulsive self-licking, self-mutilation, inappropriate aggression, excessive yowling, and tail chasing all bring the cats into clinics for thorough examinations and testing. When no medical problem can be found, veterinarians treat the animals with a program of behavior modification and perhaps even a prescription of a behavior-modifying drug. That boredom and loneliness could wreak so much havoc surprised everyone.

Sometimes, rather than express her dissatisfaction in masochism or aggression, the isolated cat begins to shut down. A cat who has lost all playfulness, facial expression, and curiosity forfeits personality. She sleeps twenty-three of her twenty-four daily hours, rising only for food and a trip to the litter box. The clichés "bored out of her mind" and "lost her mind" reflect just how the mind seems to vanish after existing in a purposeless, monotonous environment for a long period.

While our homes contain a lot of stimulation for us, they may be very dull to the cat. It's interesting to note that experimental laboratory cats living in spare conditions turn up with the same behavior problems as do indoor cats. Some lab cats pass their days in steel cages with no toys, no variety, and little interaction. While, in our eyes, the difference between our home and that cold environment is great, for the cat without much to do, the effect is about the same.

The world-famous San Diego Zoo takes environmental enrichment very seriously. In fact, their staff of behaviorists works hard to design and fill the animals' enclosures with some of the same intrigue that exists in a natural habitat. Every few days, a keeper will borrow a goat from the Children's Zoo Petting

Paddock to take to Tiger River, where the Indo-Chinese tigers roam. Before the tigers emerge for the day, the keeper leads the goat on a long path through the grasses and trees. The goat then trots back to the petting zoo, safe and sound. When the tigers come out into the morning air, they immediately lift their noses, picking up the scent. They spend two to three hours following it. During that time, their minds are engaged.

In a current project, a zoo engineer has created a large metal ball that wobbles erratically, mimicking the motion of prey. The ball will be introduced and left in the enclosures for a short period of time. The behaviorists want to pique the cats' interest but remove the device quickly enough so that its novelty remains.

These are just two of the strategies in an arsenal of ideas employed by the zoo's animal enrichment program. As Gary Priest, manager of applied animal behavior, explains, "if you had to put enrichment into two words, they would be variety and randomness." The behaviorists may introduce the ball one day, lay a scent trail down another, and hide a special food treat in the exhibit on a third. There's not one perfect enrichment, Priest explains. There has got to be a combination and a variety. In the following pages, we've provided all the variety your budget and energy level will allow.

When you're away, the cat will play—in surroundings that offer her three important things:

1. Many opportunities to make choices

2. Enticements to activity
3. An occasional random event

A brain engaged in activities that involve these factors does not have to occupy itself with compulsive, annoying, and inappropriate behavior. When reading about environmental improvements, keep in mind that cats do get used to a routine, even if that routine is not good for them. Once a cat establishes her pattern, she has a hard time changing it. If you're taking your cat from a boring environment to an exciting one, use caution. Don't simply buy out the pet supply catalogs, redecorate your house, and expect your cat to emerge from under the bed any time soon. A lot of commotion in the house, such as rearranging furniture, adding new objects, and remodeling can be very stressful to some cats, especially those who are timid or anxious in the first place. Add furnishings one at a time. Allow a few weeks between each change or addition. Open up her living area one room at a time. Give her a chance to get used to her new limits. She'll find the fun. . . slowly.

Creating Opportunities for Choice

One of the keys to keeping the cat's mind stimulated is to provide lots of opportunities to make choices. The more choices available, the more decisions must be made. In decision-making, the brain must work to evaluate all the options and come to a conclusion. This process sparks the formation of neural pathways. With a few household modifications, you can have the cat moving from room to room, picking one activity over the other all day. Given the right environment, she'll fill each day with different ways of climbing, observing, chasing, hunting, and playing.

Start by giving your cat as large a territory to roam as possible. Free-ranging domestic cats usually map out an entire acre for themselves. Your master bedroom falls short. Your cat has explored every last dust ball and window blind there. Open up as many rooms as you feel comfortable, and open the closets in those rooms as well.

Opening your house up to your cat has another advantage. The more rooms available, the more space you have to fill with challenging furnishings for her, furnishings that allow her to explore heights as well as distances. Outside, cats have various sizes of trees to climb. Sometimes they want a low branch from which to swipe at passersby. Sometimes they climb very high to put a lot of distance between themselves and their annoying cohabitants. The outdoor cat has a lot of choice of how high she wants to go and how much energy to expend to get there.

On the other hand, the inside cat's up-and-down options are limited. Many inside cats jump up on armoires or refrigerators, springing eight feet or more to these perches. But these have their limitations. To really satisfy a cat's desire to dwell in the upper strata, you can build a "catwalk" just for her. A catwalk consists of several planks six to twelve inches wide, securely affixed about two feet below the ceiling. With this walk in place, the cat can stalk the room's perimeter—only seven feet up. She can look down and observe events, gaining a new perspective.

While boards for the path are easy to come by, a stairway to reach it may be a bit tougher. Luckily, Avcon Products has created a fabulous staircase called The Kitty Walk that bolts to your wall. This narrow, ten-foot stair will take your cat from the middle of your wall (which she can easily jump to) to the lofty catwalk. The Kitty Walk comes with a square perch at the bottom and at the top of the staircase. At around $150, it's an expensive plaything, but if you're not the carpenter type, you can order from this company.

Avcon Products also makes a shorter, carpeted staircase ideal for going from the floor to the window. At $79.95, you can get it in three-, four-, and five-foot lengths. This Kitty Walk Deluxe includes a sisal scratching area, a dangling playball, and information about training the cat to climb. These perches with their ladders should be put at different heights, even in several rooms. To contact Avcon Products, write them at 10162 Orangewood Avenue, Garden Grove, CA 92640.

If your cat's aspirations transcend stair-climbing, The Climbing Net available at House of Cats International will provide the challenge she's looking for. This obstacle is a network of sturdy sisal rope knotted into two-inch squares. Stretched over a frame of natural cedar, the net is interspersed with feather toys and wooden beads. Halfway up, the cat can stop to spin a bead around. Once the cat reaches the top, she can scramble onto a cat perch you've affixed above The Climbing Net. All that effort deserves a little rest, after all. Habitual curtain climbers may be able to refocus their energies on this invention. At $30 per square foot, The Climbing Net comes made to order, as tall and as wide as you like. Contact House of Cats International at 25011 Bell Mountain Drive, San Antonio, TX 78255, or call them at 800–889–7402.

Different levels of climbing and a variety of roaming paths open new perspectives to the cat. They also allow her to express her drive to climb. She can spend the day high or low. Either way, when the day starts, she knows she has a variety of places to go and explore. In thinking about which offers the most advantages that day, she must use her mind.

After all that climbing, your cat needs a place to rest. You may think that any couch or favorite pillow will do, but if you want to maximize brainpower, have the cat rest in an area where something's going on. Cat perches made to fit in front of windows serve well. Many of us already have one, but adding another one or two multiplies the benefits. Several cat perches allow the cat to take advantage of the sunlight as it streams in the east window in the morning and the west window in the afternoon. If the cat doesn't move and enjoy the variety of views of her own volition, the sun will surely lure her from place to place. More important, when the action outside moves from the front of the house to the back, the cat can follow it. In the morning, she can watch neighbors leaving for work from the east window. In the afternoon, birds scrounging for seeds in the backyard provide plenty of viewer excitement. Pet stores and the R.C. Steele

Wholesale Pet Supply catalog stock many varieties of window perches ranging in price from $25 to $45.

So the cat has great access to the window, but what if nothing ever occurs out there? If that's the case, it's not hard to bring the show to her. One way to do this is to put a bird feeder within viewing distance. The Secret View Cat Entertainment Center consists of a lightweight bird feeder that you can affix to your window. A one-way mirror lets the bird eat peacefully while seeing only her reflection. Little does she know that on the other side of the glass, a cat is going berserk with prey drive. Secret View Cat Entertainment Center is available in pet stores and on the Internet at Acme Pet (www.acmepet.com).

Most of us would be satisfied that the cat has a few ramps to climb and window perches from which to watch the world. When you get started entertaining your cat, however, you may have a hard time stopping. For those of you who will spare no expense, elaborate kitty apartments will satisfy your desire to provide your cat with a cornucopia of activity. These multilevel activity centers keep your cat moving, batting, scratching, and climbing. At five-and-a-half feet tall, the four levels are accessed by carpeted ramps going from floor to floor. The top level contains several hanging toys, a sisal scratching post, and a real tree limb. Called the Cadillac of play centers, The Standard Environment from House of Cats International runs from $500 to $675. They also make a super-deluxe version for a mere $5,000.

Feeling tired just reading about all these possible activities? Imagine how excited and stimulated your cat will be. She won't be at a loss for things to do, even if you're not there to direct her. With abundant decisions to make, the cat's brain cells keep busy forming connections and storing fresh information. She can climb, observe the world outside of the window, even run through the levels of her kitty apartment. She'll have worn herself out, physically and mentally, all while you were gone!

Prey Facsimiles: Introducing Random Events

Providing plenty of options to choose from is only one way to keep the brain churning. We can follow that act with the real excitement: the hunt. The hunt still provides the greatest thrill and stimulation for our cats. Chasing and pouncing may look easy, but these activities require a great deal of strategy, memory, and agility.

In fact, hunting has lead carnivores to the head of the intellectual pack. Because of their diet, hunting animals (carnivores) have developed much larger, more complex brains than herbivores. Herbivores don't have to plan, chase, and outmaneuver a leafy tree. They simply get up and start munching. We're smarter because we've had to work harder. We've earned it.

During the hunt, while most of the thinking goes on in the stalking process, the lack of predictability also taxes the hunter's mind. The hunter— the cat in our case—must know where her potential dinner dwells and about what time it emerges. She must decide how to position herself in order to have the best shot at a successful capture. Once the chase begins, the cat's response is automatic. The prey object has to vary its escape trajectory wildly to evade the pursuer. By providing opportunities for our cats to stalk and pursue prey objects, we're helping them use their minds.

Short of populating your home with mice, it's tough to find a prey substitute. Only living creatures can appear randomly and change their escape routine every single time. We can, however, provide a modicum of randomness and unpredictability by combining our television sets with a common household device called an appliance timer. Appliance timers can be found in home supply and hardware stores. They are part of an extension cord that cuts and supplies the power source based on your timer settings. If you set your television to run so that it just needs the power to turn it on, you can control it even though you're not home. Set the appliance timer to run for five minutes and then shut off. To maximize the chances that the show will be something the cat is interested in, turn to the Animal Planet, the Discovery Channel, or any local channel that focuses on animals. You can even find out when appropriate shows will air. Every day, change the times the television comes on. Yesterday, other animals appeared in the morning; today, the afternoon. Skip a day. Some appliance timers can even be set to turn on the appliance several times in a twenty-four–hour period.

Despite your obvious fiddling with the television, all the cat knows is that other creatures may appear in the house at any time. She flies to the television to see what's going on. Birds and mice scamper across the screen. Since the cat may be excited, it would be wise to have a small table or chair situated in front of the television for her, so she can get close enough to bat the screen safely.

While you'll have to be around to put this next strategy in "play," your cat will enjoy it. Several companies have created videos involving cats' typical prey objects. *Video Catnip* from PetAvision comes highly recommended from cat lovers. It features prancing and dancing birds, squirrels, and chipmunks, all professionally videotaped. You can write to PetAvision at Box 102, Morgantown, WV 26507, or call 800–521–7898. The cost is $19.95, and it's twenty-five minutes long. There are several others available in pet stores and catalogs.

While there has been some debate on the practicality of feline television viewing, the last word is in: Cats can see the images on the screen. According to *Cat Watch*, a newsletter from the Cornell University College of Veterinary Medicine, cats do see television, if perhaps a bit differently than we do. Where we see smooth movement, they see jumpy images. But this difference doesn't mean cats can't enjoy their favorite shows. In fact, the television entrances many cats even more because of this erratic movement. Television is not all bad. It can entertain and enrich all of us, even our cats!

If your cat isn't the television type, however, a fish tank full of active fish affords the cat a view of creatures that move unpredictably. The cat will enjoy close access to the tank by means of a sturdy chair or table placed directly in front of it. But let's not forget the other creatures involved. For their part, the delicate fish would appreciate a tight lid over their home that's sturdy enough to hold the cat's weight. Observational access to the tank and a sturdy lid make this arrangement very safe.

Before You Leave the House: Enticements to Activity

While we're gone, we've accomplished a lot with the above adaptations. We've gotten the cat exploring, climbing, observing, and chasing. But there's no rest for the Cat Fanatic (and if you bought this book, you may have already earned that title). Before we head out for the day, we can start her morning off right by getting her moving and thinking.

Setting up a kitty treasure hunt keeps the cat engaged. First, before you leave in the morning, have someone hold the cat while you get a handful of her favorite treats or toys. Let her watch you planting these objects around the house. Place them behind a pillow, in a planter, or under a couch. If her attention wanders, try to get it back as you plant the treats so that she'll have an idea of where to find them. The first time you try this, you may want to stick around and help her locate the treats. The treasure hunt gives kitty a schedule of objects to unearth for the day. If you're concerned about putting treats on your carpet and chairs, place them on top of small paper plates. The plates will not only protect your furnishings but also help the cat see the treat. This game keeps her exploring the house, moving from one room to another, all while using her mind.

When setting up the treat treasure hunt gets old, you can easily fashion another challenge for your cat: Assignment Unpack. Some people have cats who are natural unpackers. Owners come home from work to find an entire sock drawer emptied. Kitty has spent the afternoon fishing out sock after sock until the drawer would yield no more.

These socks always need rearranging....

To make a toy similar to this activity, take an empty Kleenex box and tape it to your hardwood or tile floor with packing tape. Fill it with wadded balls of paper or a few small, lightweight rags (observe which is easier for her to extract). You can even put a treat or catnip in the bottom to entice the cat a bit. Like the treasure hunt, for her first exposure to this activity, stick around and help her remove a few of the balls. Enticing her to be active will keep her mind and body challenged even though you're not there to witness every move.

The enthusiasm with which some cats turn to activities like the above demonstrates that they're happy to work toward a goal. If that's the case, how about getting a little muscle power out of the cat when it comes to meals? The Cat Scratch Feeder by Del West Enterprises is a scratching post that dispenses food. When the cat scratches, the hollow cylindrical post pushes against a spring and food drops out. Since you control the amount of food you put into the feeder, the cat cannot overeat, no matter how much she scratches. This clever device keeps the cat focused on scratching an appropriate object—the post. It also forces her to work a little for her food. The Cat Scratch Feeder rewards a cat for scratching appropriate objects, making training easier and perhaps eliminating the need for declawing. To see the feeder, you can go to the website (www.mktmkt.com/pavlovscat.html). You can also call the manufacturer, Del West, at 619–689–9999 to find which local stores carry it.

Another great product that keeps the cat moving and exploring is the Play-N-Treat from Virtu. Place dry cat food in the small hole and watch the cat bat the toy around, trying to free that kibble! Inside the ball, the kibble tumbles over barriers that prevent it from sliding out of the hole too easily. We suggest you fill the Play-N-Treat with half of the cat's morning food ration, leaving the other half in her bowl. It will take your cat a good hour to get that last morsel out of its plastic prison. If you can't find the Play-N-Treat in your pet supply store, you can reach Virtu at 1300 East Street, Fairport Harbor, OH 44077, or call 800–565–2695. You can also check out their products on the Web (www.virtupets.com).

The key in all of these strategies is variety and novelty. We've offered a lot of ideas just so you'll have enough to keep rotating them. For instance, remember to put away the Play-N-Treat for a week, and then bring it out for two days. Fill it with half of the cat's morning food one day, three cat treats the next day, and then put it away again. You can even set up a schedule of activities. Mondays and Thursdays, the television comes on. Tuesday, you set up a kitty treat treasure hunt. Wednesday, you two take a walk outside on the leash. Having a different activity every day keeps your cat focused on you, contemplating what wonder you'll come up with next!

The Comforts of Home

When the cat's not climbing, unpacking, or exploring, she needs a nice atmosphere to relax. Many mammals are comforted by a steady stream of noise. A radio keeps background sounds consistent so that a sudden crash may not be as frightening for your sensitive pet. Leaving a radio on not only evens out the daily sound, but the human voices also comfort the cat.

When the disc jockey is quiet, the music played has some important benefits to any mammal's mind. Researchers are exploring whether music can be as effective as some drugs in improving memory. Apparently, listening to music requires the work of the same neural synapses used in memory formation. Several studies have shown that those who listen to music perform better on spatial reasoning tests. Leaving the radio on not only makes the cat's environment more enjoyable, but it may also invigorate her intellect.

When the cat needs to give her active mind a rest, a comfortable bed that's all hers is a must. The cat needs an area all her own to recharge from the stresses she has experienced. Further, if she has a bed she enjoys, she's more likely to stay away from comfy couches and expensive sweaters. To make her bed irresistible, put an expendable article of your clothing in it so she can sleep with the scent of her favorite pal.

Random events, opportunities for choice, and areas to explore—all are brain builders. These strategies help the cat occupy himself during the long hours that you are away. In implementing them, remember to change the cat's routine and environment slowly, adding one element or activity at a time, and leaving a week or two between each addition. There are many activities in this book. If you choose to use even two of them, the needle on your cat's excitement meter will swing upwards.

Getting Outdoors Safely: The Indoor Cat vs. the Outdoor Cat

If all of these strategies smack as poor substitutes for the thrill of the great outdoors, there are two ways to get your cat outside while keeping her safe and under your control. First, let's establish that cats that stay strictly indoors are more likely to avoid infectious diseases, parasites, and many types of accidents. On average, indoor cats live longer than those with access to the outside. Yet the safety enjoyed by indoor cats comes at the cost of stimulation and fun. Cats with access to the outdoors have more opportunities to express their "catness." They patrol their territorial limits, ever watchful for the intruder on the horizon. They chase and even conquer the mighty lizard or sparrow. They play with the nearest blowing leaf.

Many owners, however, do not want to risk kitty's life and health by

allowing her access to the nearest neighborhood disease, growling dog or speeding car. A possible compromise is walking your cat on a leash, much as dog owners do. Getting the cat outside has many advantages. In the fresh air, there are always new scents and sights. A walk outside gives the mind the novelty on which it thrives. In fact, many owners report that their cats follow them when they step out for a walk. Cats do enjoy walking outside. If you can get them to do it on a leash, everyone stays safe.

While cats don't respond well to collars around the neck, a harness, it seems, falls within their definition of acceptable indignity. Believe it or not, many cats come to enjoy walking on a leash. They realize it's a rare opportunity to smell, explore, and exercise, although very active and shy kitties may not adjust to harnessing. If your cat becomes distressed when the harness comes out, look for other ways to provide stimulation for her. Cats cannot be strong-armed. If you do think harness training may be an option for your cat, here's how to pull it off.

Seven Easy Steps to Harness Training Your Cat

With your gentle guidance, your cat could come to recognize the benefits of walking on a leash. These steps will help get you through the first weeks of harness and leash training.

1. Get her accustomed to the harness and leash by putting them in her living area. Allow her to examine it and get used to its smell. Drag it

across the floor and let her play with it. After batting it around a bit, she'll recognize it as non-threatening.

2. Put the harness on her and let her wear it for five to ten minutes. Then increase the amount of time she wears the harness each day for seven to ten days. The cat should not wear the harness unsupervised, because it could snag on something causing injury. If the cat puts up an immediate revolt, give in. Take the harness off and leave it in her living area again for a few days where she can inspect it at her leisure.

3. Once she's wearing the harness calmly, get her accustomed to the leash by attaching it to the harness and allowing her to drag it around for a few minutes while she is in your sight. The leash and the harness should both be as lightweight as possible.

4. Once she's calm while the leash trails her, pick up the end and hold it. If she gets up to move, follow her. Follow her wherever she goes, but help her understand you're holding the lead.

5. The tough part: getting her to respond to your motions. As you hold the leash, get her attention by calling her name and dangling a food treat a few feet in front of her. Walk forward and encourage her to walk a few steps toward the treat. When you move, the treat moves with you. If she complies, give her the food treat. Keep plying her with food until she has walked across the room with you.

6. Continue to increase the distance you entice her to walk while on the leash until she's responding well. Eventually, you should be walking from room to room together.

7. If the cat pulls on the lead, simply hold tight. Never yank her. If she moves in the wrong direction, stand still and hold the leash tight. She'll realize that it's her motions that are causing her discomfort. Once the cat moves in the direction you want, the pressure ends.

Practice in an enclosed yard or patio first, so you retain control if the cat panics. It may take a while for you to get around the block or even down the driveway. If your cat has never been outside, it's particularly important to take small steps into the big world. Rest assured that leash training can be done. It *is* done. In Chapter Seven: The Wise Elder, we discuss more in depth how to train a cat to respond to your commands.

Keep in mind that harness training your cat to go outside is just one strategy in an arsenal of methods to keep your cat engaged and excited about her environment. If you provide an exciting environment inside the house, you don't need to feel guilty over the fact that your cat can't go outside.

Patio Living for the Indoor Cat

Another way to get the cat outside safely is to build a screened-in patio just for her. We don't have to let the cat in on the fact that her "patio" is just an oversized cage. Cat patios that keep their occupants happiest tend to be at least five feet wide and ten feet long. They contain real tree branches covered with thick scratchable bark. Several perches at different levels please the cat as well. If you don't have perches, cushioned patio furniture also provides an acceptable elevated view. While the cat patio can be a freestanding structure in your yard, it's usually most convenient for everyone when attached to the home. When building your patio, remember to provide a large enough door so you can get in. A cat patio connected to the house needs a cat door so your pet can run inside in case of rain or any other threats. A strong screen or even fencing keeps out most predators. Before you buy your building materials, make sure you know your local predators and what they are capable of getting under and through.

The intellectual benefits of patio living aren't to be sneezed at. On the patio, cats can enjoy the antics of the birds and any neighbors visible. Even when nothing is going on, the change of scenery does them good. They appreciate the smells that waft their way and listen to all the sounds of life prevalent in your area. People that have cat patios find their cats spend the majority of their time there. If you think your cat would appreciate some fresh air and new sights, this outdoor cage may be the answer. While no one in your neighborhood may have a cat patio, rest assured that many owners across the country are indulging their pets in this way. (In other words, you're not the only cat nut.)

The Ultimate Activity: A Kitty Friend

All of these strategies help, but no perch, catwalk, or patio can be as stimulating to your cat as another living, breathing creature in the home.

Only another cat can play with the expertise and energy your cat needs. Veterinarians report that some abnormal cat behaviors vanish once the owner brings home a friend for her.

But aren't cats solitary? Yes and no. Because their prey (mice, birds, lizards) are small, wild cats usually don't need to form packs to conquer them as dogs and wolves do. With field mice and birds weighing so little, one cat takes care of the job quite well.

Unlike wild canines, small wild cats have the best chances of survival if they dominate a territory by themselves. Alone, they have access to all the

Hurry! *The X-Files* is starting!

creatures skittering across the landscape. Nature makes survival an iffy thing. Whether a life of solitude is actually their preference is another question. Because it's a necessity doesn't mean it's a desire.

We can find insight into what cats truly prefer by observing cat societies where plenty of food is available. Under these conditions, cats form close communities. A prime example involves farm cats, whose communities can reach twenty or thirty. These cooperative felines organize to help one another. Mother cats care for one another's litters and even nurse another's kittens. They're also great baby-sitters. When one cat hunts, another takes care of the kittens. These societies are usually made up of many female cats and one male cat. While the females help one another out, they also curry favor with the male and like to sleep close to him, even if they're not in heat. While the existence of a strict hierarchy is unclear, it appears that the male acts as the dominant cat of the group, while the subordinate cats have equal status. Any other male cat wandering into the compound either deposes the current male or is fought off by him. When conditions are good and survival isn't paramount, cats enjoy and benefit from working together and entertaining one another.

Giving your cat a same-species companion has many benefits. Dr. Michael Fox reports that many of the healthiest cats he sees in his practice come from homes where another cat dwells. In fact, when a companion dies, many cats go through a clear and indisputable grieving period. A particularly traumatic bereavement can incite the cat to stop eating or engage in destructive behavior. Some cats even slink off to avoid contact with all humans and animals after a loved one has died. This conduct often lasts for months and can even be the cat's *modus operandi* until its own death. Any cat owner who has had one cat die leaving a survivor behind knows that cats appreciate each other's company and can mourn the loss of it.

Why is it so valuable to have a playmate with the same number of legs? Playing as only cats can play, grooming and exploring, all enable cats to express their natural drives. For wild felines, play is a dress rehearsal for the more serious activities in life. Since nothing so serious as actual self-sufficiency will ever come our cats' way, play provides one of the few challenges available to them. With more play, physique improves. Vigorous play that only another can provide—rolling, chasing, wrestling—stimulates circulation and improves heart function and muscle tone. A solitary ten-year-old cat may have forgone playing completely. On the other hand, owners of two ten-year-old cats often report that their pets still play regularly.

Two cats together also stimulate each other's minds. A cat wrestling match enhances problem-solving abilities. In a shot at mock-triumph, they are forced to find ways to vanquish each other. They push each other to the ground, wrestle over toys, and try to outrun each other. They explore more. One alerts the other to the presence of treacherous trespassers, such as spiders. Together, they double-team these intruders. When one discovers something interesting, the other is not far behind. Another cat can bring excitement to your cat's life in many ways.

While living in Santa Fe, New Mexico, Carol Peacocke shared a household with Spike and Molly, littermates who were fast friends. Not only did these two eat, play, and sleep together, but they also helped each other torment the neighbor's Siberian husky. While smaller, they had an unfair advantage: The dog was tied securely in the yard on a lead. Spike would sit a couple of inches away from the farthest point the dog could reach and Molly, behind him, would run back and forth, egging the dog on. Carol and her family could see Spike's head turning left and right, calmly observing the dog's frantic attempts to free himself and chase them. This torture ended only when the cats got bored and headed into the house for a nap. They needed to rest up so that they could resume the game the next day.

Mine, all mine!

Despite the benefits most cats receive from having a same-species companion, there are those cats who really and truly want to be an only kitty. You'll discover whether this is your cat's mind-set if the introduction of a second cat prompts the first cat to spray your entire set of linen drapes. Once a possessive first cat latches on to a human that loves them, they aren't gonna share—no way, no how. Further, cats have such strictly defined borders of their territory, they may decide your home isn't big enough for another.

Those thinking of getting a second cat should take some precautions. According to Dr. Michael Fox and other cat experts, a second cat coming into the home is more welcomed when he's a kitten and the opposite sex of the first cat. These parameters make the new addition less threatening. If your second cat is a kitten, have a separate pen or place for her for the first two months when you are not home. Kittens can annoy an adult cat to the scratching point. Initially, kittens cannot handle as much space as your adult cat.

Once you get your second cat, you'll want to quarantine her for two weeks. Of course, you can interact with the cat, but make sure to keep any other household pets away from her. Take the cat for an examination by a veterinarian right away. The veterinarian will test for feline viruses and external and internal parasites, which could be passed along to other cats. If the cat is clear of all these problems, upper respiratory germs may still be lurking, ready to give your kitty a nasty cold. The two-week isolation gives these germs a chance to make their presence known. The quarantine also allows time to let the cats adjust to each other's scents and sounds before they have to be bombarded with each other's looks and antics as well. After two weeks the cats can be introduced with supervision for five or ten minutes at a time. Dr. Wayne Hunthausen, past president of the American Veterinary Society of Animal Behavior, suggests owners introduce the cats in a large room. That way our skittish pets can have lots of options of where to run and hide if the urge strikes.

Over the next week, you can gradually increase supervised interaction. If fighting does not occur, reward both cats with treats and encourage interactive play behavior.

If fighting does occur, separate the cats immediately. Cats that don't get along should always be separated when you cannot supervise them. As in all conflicts, one cat is usually more aggressive than the other. Veterinary behaviorist Dr. Karen Overall advises clients to put the aggressor in a "less desirable space." The more passive cat should get the fun rooms. Be close on hand when the cats are together. When either cat shows any sign of aggression, the owner needs to intervene by startling her with a loud noise, a spray from a water gun, or a puff of air in the face. Break up fighting cats by throwing a blanket over them. Don't try to referee them yourself.

Even if your cats don't actually come to blows, you may find your household could still be more pleasant. Food can help. Using a treat or kibble, you can ease the two curmudgeons within pacing distance of each other. For long-term friendliness, you can help the cats get accustomed to each other by letting them eat together. Start with the food dishes at a distance where the cats can see each other, but can still eat without getting upset. Each day move the dishes a little closer together.

If food doesn't generate friendliness, a new synthetic pheromone spray from Abbott Laboratories might. Initially developed to decrease urine-spraying, Feliway has been effective in calming cats in many kinds of stressful situations. Feliway is available through your veterinarian.

In Short. . .

Filling your cat's environment with excitement and challenge can do wonders for her mind, mood, and energy level. At the University of Illinois, psychologist and cell biologist Dr. William Greenough found that rats exposed to an enriched environment experienced a sudden surge of neural growth after the experience. The numbers are impressive. These rodents had 25 percent more connections between brain cells than they did before they stepped into their souped-up playground.

A cat who has spent the day playing, exploring, and observing the neighborhood is a brighter, happier, more well-adjusted pet. Remember to vary your stimulation strategies. One day you can arrange Assignment Unpack. The next day hide treats around the house for her. On the third day, set your television up to turn on. She'll thrill in all the variety you offer. The San Diego zookeepers do exactly this, only on a larger scale. While your cat may never become a witty dinner guest, she will be more alert, curious, and interesting. You, too, feel more satisfied that you're doing all you can to give your cat a fulfilling life.

4

Games and Toys to Keep the Mind Purring

Remember that doctor game you played as a kid? (Admit it: You did it.) You may be tempted to write it off as a childish way to explore, but that game and all other forms of play are designed for a serious purpose. Experts explain that play prepares juveniles of every species for adult responsibilities. Human children prepare to bake, repair cars, doctor, nurse, and mother with products from Fisher-Price. Rounds of playing pretend family, make-believe store, and imaginary romance all enable us to practice these complex tasks before the time comes that we must actually perform them.

So when your cat attacks your bare toes, smile and be glad. Instinct is preparing him to maul your entire body when he's older. Kittens kill the hours practicing their right hooks, head butts, and neck holds with their siblings. This hard work, while it looks fun now, eventually teaches the cat to fight, hunt, and kill. Playing kittens don't register that they'll never need to chase down any mice, because our cabinets sag with gourmet cat food. Cats, smart as they are, have hitched a ride with some generous Sugar Daddies and Mommies. They are responsibility-free.

That freedom, however, is the very reason adult indoor cats need games and toys. Playing games with us and with their toys brings a modicum of challenge to their cushy lives. Regular play keeps the cat's mind and body agile. Rolling, chasing, and wrestling all stimulate circulation and improve heart function, balance, and muscle tone. Although we love our cats for their intellect, we shouldn't neglect their bodies.

Play also tones our cats' minds. A whirling feather toy keeps him anticipating which path the flying plume might take next. Playing hide-and-seek with you forces him to develop escape and hunt strategies. Playing (either with games or toys) provides your cat an outlet for his tendencies to plan, hunt, and conquer. Without them, the cat doesn't have much to think about, except for that next meal.

Sometimes cats create their own games. Spike and Molly, Carol Peacocke's cats mentioned in the previous chapter, managed a little ingenuity. After teasing the neighbor's dog in the morning, they would condescend to come in—but not without bringing a bit of nature with them. Both cats carried in injured mice, large beetles, and spiders, which they took straight to the bathroom. Unable to escape, the creatures would scramble madly at the sides of the tub while the cats batted them back and forth between each other. Most often the bugs or mice would be rescued by a horrified household human. It was no secret that Spike and Molly enjoyed this game tremendously. Partly because of the fun they had, the two pals remained bright and active their entire lives.

Play provides more benefits than physical and mental stimulation. It also bonds cat and owner. Games help us explore each other's sense of humor, energy level, likes, and dislikes. The better we know each other, the closer we become. Playing enables us to explore our cats' potential as well as our own.

Types of Cat Play: Social vs. Object

To provide our cats the most satisfying play experience, we must explore just why and how they play. Cats have two styles of play—social and object play—which help them acquire certain survival skills. Social play teaches them how to fight, escape threatening cats, and pursue mice and birds. It consists of pouncing, hiding, chasing, and mimicking the postures of offense and defense. The gymnastics involved in social play develop physical fitness, coordination, and balance.

The hard work of social play occurs most intensely before the age of seven weeks, when other kittens are still available to play with. Kittens stand on their rear legs and bat at each other. They roll around on the floor, front paws clasped around each other's necks. Since social play involves another, it's best to allow kitty to learn the lessons taught by social play with its littermates. Leaving the kitten with its family until ten to twelve weeks ensures that he will learn these important lessons in the most appropriate setting.

Adult cats continue to engage in social play, although not as frequently. It's tough for human owners to meet this need, since the game is physical. In the tussle, the cat usually ends up scratching the owner. Some owners, however, use a stuffed animal as a surrogate. Others put two thick socks over their hand and wrestle with their cats that way. These strategies will work if the cat keeps his claws on the inanimate fur and away from your flesh. With these intermediaries, the cat gets to rear up and spar, bite, and scratch in this mock battle to the death.

If these alternatives seem too risky, there is also a nice puppet available from Rom Designs called Harum Scarum. The padding on this creature protects your hand, and its furry body extends almost to your elbow. It's fabric tongue contains catnip, which entices the cat. Rom Designs is located at 1717 Van Buren, St. Paul, MN 55104, and can be reached at 612–644–0433.

Makayla Hoppe of Escondido, California, satisfies the need her cat, Annie, has for social play by playing hide-and-seek with her. The game seems to have some very strict rules. Makayla knows Annie is in the mood for hide-and-seek when the cat crouches and emits a low growl, putting her ears flat. On another day, Annie might even hide behind some-

He'll never find me in here!

thing, lifting her head up to establish eye contact. To join the game, Makayla must hide behind a corner and peak out, initiate eye contact and then duck behind the corner again. Since Annie gets more involved if the game is played on her level, Makayla usually plays the game on her hands and knees. Each time Makayla peeks out, Annie has moved a few steps closer. Their meeting eyes freeze both participants. Annie uses other furniture to shield her as she moves toward her owner. When Annie gets very close, she loses all inhibition and races toward Makayla. A rough growl from Makayla sends Annie leaping into the air before she can get her paws on human flesh. Makayla hides again, and the whole process repeats until one of the participants gets bored.

This fun pastime counts as social play. Hiding and peeking excite a cat because mice and other rodents do exactly this when determining whether to emerge from the safety of their burrow. How many nature shows have you seen where the poor little mouse pokes a nose out of his hole to make sure the horizon is feline-free? Hide-and-seek enables the cat to romp heartily with another being.

However you satisfy your cat's drive for social play, make sure innocent fun doesn't escalate into aggression. Watching a human run away gives some cats the idea that they are the ruling animal in the household. Cats who get this chip on their shoulders usually tend toward dominance anyway. If the playing cat starts growling, hissing, or stalking and attacking when you aren't prepared, stop the fun immediately. Start practicing some of the strategies for combating dominance described in Chapter Two: Kitten Kindergarten.

While the above strategies may serve the purpose of social play, the best provider is another cat. Only another cat can understand how your cat wants to cavort. Chapter Three: Home Alone covers the benefits of the two-cat household.

Object Play: Bring Out the Toys!

Where another creature serves as the focus in social play, objects (toys) get all the attention in object play. In a fight (trained for in juvenile social play), a cat is evenly matched. In a hunt (trained for in juvenile object play), the mouse is blatantly overmatched. Because we like to keep the local mice outside our house, toys are the best we have to stand in as easily manipulated, small prey targets for our domestic cats. Cats scoop, toss, bat, grasp, bite, pounce, and chase the poor victim, exerting all their hunting skills on innocent Ping-Pong balls or catnip mice.

To ensure our cats are interested in the toys we choose, we must ask ourselves: How can we make toys come closest to the actions and shapes of natural prey objects? Since mice constitute the cat's most common meal, we'll analyze the habits of these creatures.

Emerging from holes and brush, a mouse seems to come from nowhere. It rarely runs in a straight line but zigzags in a desperate attempt to lose its pursuer. To get its paw on a mouse, the cat often pulls it from holes or chases it through an obstacle course over an unpredictable route. Stealthy stalking and an unexpected pounce are also skills the cat utilizes. Once the mouse is caught, the cat quickly learns that each mouse varies in weight and ability. With the variability inherent in all of these factors, hunting a mouse is more of a challenge than it appears. The novelty and unexpectedness give the cat plenty of thrill.

We can simulate these challenges with toys and other devices. In looking for a fun toy for your cat, keep these three elements in mind:

1. Make sure the toy moves unpredictably. Erratic, nonlinear movement is more thrilling than a straight, predictable retreat. A mouse trying to lose a cat doesn't pick a point in the distance and dash straight to it. It darts right and left, hoping to shake the bigger animal on the sharp turns.

2. Keep the toys small and light so that they can go as far as possible. A lightweight toy rolls a lot farther when batted. Our cats are not very strong, and their natural prey is not very large.

3. Remember to watch for anything passing through your house that could serve as a toy. Novelty keeps our cats excited. The best way to keep a lot of new toys rolling in and out of a cat's life is to convert what you would normally throw away into a toy. Otherwise you need to get used to buying new toys on a regular basis. Novelty invigorates.

Homemade Toys That Satisfy

While pet stores contain toys that do meet our three criteria, it's not difficult to find household objects and items you'd normally throw away to create toys appropriate for your cat's needs. The list includes plastic milk caps, a crumpled piece of paper, boxes, large paper bags, baskets, racquetballs, Ping-Pong balls, bottle caps (without sharp edges), paper cups, and film containers with a bell placed inside. A cardboard cylinder from toilet paper will roll easily, as does a ball of yarn. You can enhance a knotted sock with catnip. Bubbles, too, are inexpensive and fun for some cats. Yarn and any type of string can be ingested, however, so you must supervise when your cat is playing with these things. Coauthor Dr. Ribarich has surgically removed several feet of string, Christmas tinsel, and even curling ribbon from the intestines of various cats.

A cat can accidentally swallow the end of a string. Because of his coarse tongue, his efforts to spit the string out will backfire, and he'll end up ingesting more. String and ribbon can also get wrapped around the base of the cat's tongue. While string may look innocent, beware its harmful potential.

To make toys more interesting, you can suspend them with a small Slinky. Plastic Slinkys, which come in all shapes and sizes these days, enable a toy to gyrate wildly. You simply need to tape one end under the table and affix a toy or ball to the other. Watch as the cat reaches up to pull on it. It will spring back and fly erratically.

After mentioning all of these toys, we must admit that the cat's most beloved toy is the modified fishing rod. This, too, can be made easily from household materials. Simply tie fishing line or string to any kind of short pole or dowel you have laying around the house. The stick of a plunger will do. Tie a piece of material, paper, or a feather at the other end and you've created an airborne bird, darting in any direction you happen to flick your wrist. These toys provide the erratic movement that hypnotizes the cat. Again, keep this and any toy involving string out of reach when you're not present.

In the wild, cats are sometimes forced to paw their way into long mouse holes. It's not surprising then that our domestic cats like to paw through a narrow tunnel and snatch a retreating object. You can simulate this experience with a flat box and a Ping-Pong ball. Measure the circumference of the Ping-Pong ball. Cut a few holes into the box, making certain that the holes are smaller than the ball so that it cannot come out. Place the ball inside the box and tape the box shut. The ball will never come out, but your cat will go nuts trying to get at it.

When raiding the garbage can, make sure to leave some dangerous objects for the trash truck. Cellophane, rubber bands, foil, thread, string, ribbon, buttons, beads, and bells can all be inadvertently ingested during play and damage a cat's intestines or become lodged in his stomach. Don't take the cat's word for it. They love to play with these castoffs and go to great lengths to convince you that nothing's wrong with them.

Be aware that your cat may take a shine to one toy and carry it around from place to place. This is normal. Wild cats carry their slain prey about with them before they actually take the first bite.

No Time for Creativity? Just Buy the Toys

If you'd like to avoid pawing over banana peels and coffee grounds in your garbage for your cat's next toy, the Frugality Police won't nab you for actually spending some money.

Cats Domino at around seven dollars allows a cat to fish inside a box to get a ball, as described above. This clever design, however, has a fulcrum in the middle, which keeps the ball rolling from one end of the flat cardboard box to the other. It's available at Designer Products Inc. Write to Box 201177, Arlington, TX 76006, or call 817–469–9416.

The urge to snake a long arm down a narrow tunnel is also satisfied by the balls ensconced in plastic tracks available in many pet supply stores. In these, the cat bats the ball around a circular tube. These products keep most cats busy for a decent period of time.

Several companies make light balls that roll well and move erratically. A company called Lixit claims to make balls that are the lightest in the business. The less weight, the further they go with a good swat. A package of three costs around four dollars. Contact Lixit at Box 2580, Napa, CA 94588, or call 707–252–1622, to find where their products are sold.

Metropolitan Pet makes House Scooters, crinkled, lightweight Mylar balls that crunch when hit. Their address is 354 Oaktree Drive, Mountain View, CA 94940, and their phone is 800–966–1819. A package of four is available for around five dollars.

Classic Products make Crinkle Puffs, balls made of a fuzzy fabric and another material that crinkles at the slightest touch. Contact them at 1451 Vanguard Drive, Oxnard, CA 93033, or 805–487–6227.

Not quite balls, but just as fun, Kookie Kitty Kurls slip in strange directions when the cat pounces on them. They're made from curled plastic, so they roll and bounce unpredictably. Find them through Omega Products, 292 Old Dover Road, Rochester, NH 03867, or call 800–258–7148.

Another wildly erratic ball is the Zig-N-Zag Ball by Virtu. Its design allows it to store energy during the initial roll. Then it rolls in an unpredictable pattern, keeping the cat guessing. If you can't find the Zig-N-Zag

Ball in your pet supply store, you can reach Virtu at 1300 East Street, Fairport Harbor, OH 44077, or call 800–565–2695. You can also check out their products on the Web (www.virtupets.com).

The Cat-O-Sphere offers a little more enticement for cats that need it. It's made of three lightweight rings that form a sphere. Inside the rings a plastic ball is suspended by a string holding it to both sides of the sphere. The inner ball is filled with catnip. For this product, write to UPCO, 3705 Pear Street, St. Joseph, MO 64502, or call 800–254–8726.

One really challenging toy requires great balance. The Tiger Toy is a clever arrangement of rope, rods, and balls suspended from the ceiling or a table. Circuses use a larger version of this product to entertain their performing Bengal tigers. Weighted balls on the ends of the rods keep the toy bouncing wildly with each attack from your cat. The erratic movement here will keep your cat guessing. Get it through Pet Door USA Inc. at 4523 30th Street West, Bradenton, FL 34207, or call 800–749–9609.

To satisfy an inquisitive mind, make sure to have different types of toys. Even if you cat's favorite toy is a cloth mouse, try to interest him in feathers and plastic toys. Give him quiet toys as well as toys with bells or crinkly noises incorporated in them. Find toy mice and birds as well as simple balls. Use catnip toys and toys without aromatic enhancement. Keep the variety going in whatever way you can.

Another way to turn toys into a mental workout is to enhance them with food. Forcing the cat to work a little for a snack will exercise his mind.

Remember, he's used to having dinner put in front of him—no thought power required there. With the toy explained below, he's forced to paw and pounce to win his snack. The bobcat must think hard to catch a mouse. Making a snack tough to get doesn't constitute teasing. Rather, it intrigues and excites our pets.

You'll need a toilet paper roll, empty tissue box, or any small box and some cat food or treats. Study the size of the food you're using. Cut several holes in the roll or box smaller than that piece. Then cut one or two holes a bit larger than the piece. Put a few pieces of food in the hole and make sure the container is otherwise sealed. Show it to your cat, and make sure that he understands he can get the food out. To demonstrate, roll it on the floor for him until one piece falls out. It's best to introduce this toy during the cat's usual feeding time so that he's motivated to attempt it. If you're not good with scissors, there's a commercial version of this toy. The Play-N-Treat by Virtu described in Chapter Three: Home Alone is a plastic ball that lets food drop out, one piece at a time.

Beyond the mental stimulation cats receive from working for their treats, food-enhanced toys can even ease behavior problems. Focused on an appropriate object, the cat doesn't have the time to consider destroying your new drapes. With a few food-enhanced toys lying around, you can bet your cat will give up a bit of his nap time to tackle them.

Cat Games

We have to be creative in finding stimulating games we can play with our cats. Beside the description of each game is an icon indicating which aspect of intelligence the game inspires. While most cats won't overtire themselves, watch for panting. That's a sign the cat has had enough, whether he will admit it or not. Cats can begin to lose coordination when they exhaust themselves. They may jump but miss their destination. These signs tell you to end the games soon. If panting or lethargy occurs early in the game, it's best to have your veterinarian examine the cat to rule out any underlying medical condition.

Remember, novelty was one of the keys to a brain that constantly develops more connections, flexibility, insight, and memory. Most owners simply resort to a few twitches of the fishing-pole toy for their cats. The novelty in that exercise wore off after about a week of that game. By learning a few new games, you can keep your cat's mind growing.

Am I being clear?

How do we know when a cat is ready to play? A cat walking back and forth on your newspaper or keyboard is trying to get you to do something to entertain him. Also, beware of a tail with a curve at the top. It can even go as far as looking like an upside-down L. Dr. Fox believes that this can be an enticement to play. Finally, if your cat throws himself down on his side in front of you, he's itching to frolic.

Cats are as individual as we are. Some are frenetic maniacs; others like more intellectual challenges. Coauthor Dr. Ribarich's older cat, Cookie, occasionally likes to bat around a tiny ball of paper. Cookie's housemate, Jake, a natural acrobat, leaps in the air to snatch a feather toy. Where Cookie learns a lot of tricks quickly, Jake's strength is athleticism. Each cat has his own predilections. When trying these games, don't give up too quickly. One game may bore the cat thoroughly, where another will energize him.

Since cats are active in the early evening, before dinner is a good time to play. Lots of cats, however, join the family for a game after the chaos of dinner ends and people are relaxing in front of the television. He has saved his energy for you, so you may as well take advantage of it.

The following icons are used to indicate which aspect of intelligence is inspired by each of the games discussed below:

problem solving   learning ability   memory

HIDE-AND-SEEK, VERSION II

In our discussion of social play, we covered one hide-and-seek game. This fun pastime has many incarnations. If you manage to get your cat to learn to stay (Chapter Five: Trick Training to Increase Brainpower), make him remain in one room. If he won't stay, you may need someone to hold him. Walk away, letting him see that you're taking his favorite treats with you. Go into another room and hide. Call him. He'll have to hunt through the house to find you. Don't think this exercise is too tough for him. He'll come to learn your favorite hiding places pretty quickly. After all, there are only so many places you can fit! Reward him with the treat once he finds you.

THE TOY CHALLENGE

Show your cat a new toy or one of his favorites. Let him play with it—but only for a moment. Take it away and place it on a bookshelf, behind a pillow, or under a couch where he can still see it but must struggle to retrieve it. Once he does get it, make the game more fun by rewarding him with a treat.

THE SHELL GAME

Three paper cups and a treat are all this game requires. The cat easily topples the paper cups. Letting the cat watch you, line the three cups up in front of him. You may need to restrain him by holding him or putting him in a sit. Put the cups far enough away so that he doesn't bat them over before you're ready. Choose one of the cups and place the treat under it. Let the cat sniff around and get the treat under the cup.

BOUNCE THAT PAPER BALL

You probably already know that your cat loves to chase a lightweight, easily batted ball of paper. The ball of paper moves erratically, as prey moves, for as long as its trajectory lasts. Throw it up or down the staircase or against a wall. (One cat we know won't condescend to chase the ball unless it has hit the wall first.) A ricochet is most exciting. The bathtub is a fun place for nimble cats to play. Batted between the sides of the tub, the ball keeps moving, often erratically.

THE HIDDEN TOY (FOR CATNIP LOVERS ONLY)

Wave the catnip toy around the room to get the scent up. When your cat comes in, put the toy behind some object: a table leg, under the couch, in the magazine rack. Encourage the kitty to look for it.

BURROWING BALL

Many owners report that their cats look away from a toy, bored, until they put it under a sheet or towel. Then the cat comes alive, interested in the unexpected behavior of the object under the cover. The sheet obliterates the prey object's true appearance, adding an element of the unknown, and the unknown is always more enticing.

An easy way to provide this fun is to attach a string to a plastic practice golf ball. The advantage of using a practice golf ball is that the holes make it easy to tie the string to. You can also use a cork, a milk cap, or anything the kitty particularly loves. After you've tied a string or fishing line to the object, throw a cover (sheet, towel, thin rug) on the floor. The cover should be thin enough to allow the cat to see the traveling object well. Put the object on one side of the cover, thread the string under the sheet and hold it at the other end. Pull the object slowly through as the cat pounces on it. Just when he thinks he has it, pull it away again. Here the "prey" becomes more of a challenge. Once again, never leave toys with strings available for the cat when you're not present.

FETCH

Cats that just don't want to retrieve won't. But many do. You'll only know if you try. In the early evening, get a toy your cat enjoys in particular. Throw it a short distance. If he picks it up and brings it back to you, you can

Ready? Fetch!

You've got to be kidding!

continue to increase the distance you throw. Reward the cat with a treat if he brings back the toy. This generosity reinforces his carrying the ball back to you, and you won't have to work so hard.

LIGHT/LASER BEAM SCAMPER

Again, some cats respond to this one and others don't. Many people, exhausted from a day's work, turn the lights down and collapse on the couch with a flashlight. They can get their cat running by shining the flashlight over the floor and moving the beam about erratically. An advance on this old flashlight idea is the Lazer Mouse by Smart Inventions. A narrow, red beam of light forms a spot on your floor or wall. Because the image is smaller, it's easier to control than your usual flashlight beam. Plus, the focused spot is closer to the size of a cat's natural prey than a flashlight orb. You can find more information on the Web (www.lazermouse.com) or call 800–275–7494.

AFGHAN OVER KITTY

If kitty is in the playing mode, one way to take advantage of his sense of humor is to throw an afghan over him. He'll be forced to tunnel his way out. Don't be surprised, though, if he asks for a pillow and settles in for a cozy nap.

PAWING FOR TOYS

Children's toy stores have plenty of little windup toys meant to join babies in the bathtub. Little do they know that cats love them as well. When avoiding the tub walls, these toys do a pretty good job of moving in an unpredictable path. Place a pan of shallow water on a linoleum or tile surface. Fill it with no more than two inches of water. (Err on the side of caution—we don't want any drowned cats.) Some regular floating toys may keep the cat's interest for a while, but make sure they're small enough for him to manipulate and even pull out of the water. Some people even put fruit and vegetable slices in the water for the kitty to bat at. They float well and some cats eat them if they manage to pluck them out in one piece.

RAMP ROLL

Can you get your hands on a panel that's a few feet wide and long? If so, lean it against your couch and move your coffee table out of the way. Sit with your cat on the floor, and roll his favorite toy up the ramp, in the way that you would play Skeeball. The cat will watch the toy's erratic trajectory and plan where to pounce once it returns to the floor.

BAT THAT BALL

Will Greenway of Chula Vista, California, stumbled across this cat game as a semisadistic eight-year-old. One day, the family cat was lying on her side on the kitchen floor. Greenway came tripping in with a handful of marbles. Eyeing an opportunity, he rolled one of the marbles at the cat's belly. Instead of getting frightened or angry as the young Greenway had gleefully expected, the cat swatted the ball right back to him. This kept both busy for a while, and the two played the game throughout the cat's life. Coauthor Suzanne Delzio's cat, Tex, plays this game with crumpled balls of paper or the lightweight balls sold in pet stores. While he enjoys it greatly, his attention span is short, so the game doesn't usually last more than ten minutes.

In Short. . .

The games and toys recommended in this chapter help to reanimate a bored and unchallenged cat. Games and toys allow the cat to practice his pounces, flex his stalking ability and challenge his strategic skills. The more you play, the more you'll want to play. You'll find that the two of you will make modifications to the games to suit your own play style. A smart idea is to give yourself a schedule. After dinner is playtime for kitty. Get into a play habit so that the cat can depend on it as well. Keep toys handy, so when the mood strikes either of you, an innocent toy lies ready to be attacked. The fun you provide for your cat will seep into your own life. Cats and their owners could all use a little more unstructured, pointless frolic.

5

Trick Training to Increase Brainpower

What's the point of training a cat? How about revenge?

Up until now, your cat has been training you. Pet me. Feed me. Lavish me with all the goodies in the pet store. You respond with a smart hop-to. It's time to get a little effort from the cat.

While almost every dog can get his fanny on the ground for a "sit," most cats slink past all our requests. They're clever. Unlike dogs, cats know to stay out of trouble in public. Because they control themselves, we don't need to bark orders at them. But training your cat brings more rewards than its usual purpose of containment and control.

Training brings a touch of challenge back to the lives of our spoiled darlings. With food and shelter delivered to them every day, our cats have no demands on them, no challenges to match their skills to. Challenge is not a bad thing. Because wild cats have spent centuries struggling for meals and territory, their brains now outweigh and outpower those of domestic cats (based on a body weight to size ratio). Over the generations, ever increasing coddling has enabled our domestic cats to avoid strenuous thought. In other words, that mangy bobcat you scared away from your trash last night could defeat your cat in a simple spelling bee. Training provides new skills that excite and stimulate the cat's mind—and it *can* be done.

In fact, Las Vegas performer Gregory Popovich does it very well. In this city of grandiose, unusual attractions, Popovich's show "Cat Skills" rivets the attention of Circus Circus Resort guests. The trainer's star, a male named Tolstoy, pushes a small dog in a baby carriage and then concludes the act by riding the dog offstage. Popovich's other feline performers jump through hoops, swing on trapezes, and wave to the audience. Were these accomplished cats specially bred and raised? No. Although at this point Popovich starts with young cats, his first successfully trained cats were shaggy souls rescued from the animal shelter.

It's not just those looking to make a buck who train their cats. Coauthor

Dr. Ribarich's cat Cookie performs reliable comes, sits, stands, downs, and rollovers. Dr. Ribarich found training unbelievably easy. There was, however, an extenuating circumstance: Cookie was on a weight reduction diet and very food-motivated at the time. After just two short practice sessions, Cookie clearly recognized what was being asked of her. Even if Dr. Ribarich doesn't request these behaviors for several weeks, Cookie can still perform perfectly (when she's in the mood).

Mike Robertson, a businessman in San Diego, California, has done the veterinarian one better. He taught his cat to fall over when he points a finger at her and says, "Bang, you're dead." We've made sure to include this impressive feat in our chapter. Cases like these prove that cats can master fun tasks—when someone takes the time to teach them.

Owners report that cats become better pets once challenged to master new tasks. Whether these tasks are stunning tricks or practical behavior guidelines aimed at making the cat a decent household citizen, they help make the kitty more enjoyable. A little learning may ease the puzzling and destructive habits common among bored cats. With her energy and curiosity directed to jumping through hoops or rolling over, getting into trouble doesn't hold as much appeal.

If tricks don't interest you, training the cat to be a decent pet shows her which behaviors you'll tolerate and which you won't. So many cats end up in the shelter because they scratch furniture or jump onto the counters, tearing into owners' favorite foods. Teaching the cat to use a scratching post and to stay off counters and away from precious objects increases the chances that she'll be viewed as a positive, *long-term* addition to the family.

The behavioral improvements owners and veterinarians see in trained cats aren't just imagined. Scientists have found that the process of training actually creates physical improvements in the animal's brain. Fresh games and toys are not the only devices that stimulate. Several studies have shown that, when an animal learns a new task, new connections are formed between nerve cells. As mentioned earlier, the more connections, the faster and stronger the brain.

One study proving this point comes from Rockefeller University. As reported in Ronald Kotulak's *Inside the Brain,* neuroscientist Dr. Hiroshi Asanuma trained monkeys to catch a ball made of food pellets. If the monkey caught the ball, he could eat it, getting his reward. If he didn't catch it, it would drop beyond his reach. It was in the monkey's best interests to learn to catch the ball. Upon studying the brain tissue of these monkeys, Asanuma found that there had been a 25 percent increase in the number of neural connections joining the sensory cortex (which enabled *seeing* the ball) with the motor cortex (which enabled *catching* the ball). These new connections make the next challenge easier to master. Learning a simple task turned the monkey's brain into a better-functioning machine.

Based on studies like this, neurosurgeons now encourage people who want to remain mentally sharp into old age to continue acquiring new skills. In fact, a separate study conducted at Columbia University by Dr. Yaakov

Stern revealed that education and interesting work could actually guard some from Alzheimer's disease. This stunning finding supports how the proper environment and activities one engages in shapes and protects the brain.

But you didn't buy your cat to become *Jeopardy* champion. Increased intelligence is not the only benefit training affords. Some veterinarians find that pets with satisfying, engaging lifestyles have a better chance of avoiding common illnesses. A cat that is active in training burns off more calories and thereby avoids obesity, a condition that contributes to threatening ailments. Demanding your cat work a little for her kibbles keeps her health in top form.

If all these benefits haven't convinced you to train your cat, hold on for one more. Training enriches the cat's emotional life because it strengthens the bond between the two of you. In training, the cat hears lots of "good kitty!" and gets petted. Spending time challenging her can help you understand her potential. Just what can she comprehend? How willing is she to do your bidding? How quickly can she learn? Similarly, with more input from you, she'll more easily understand your words and hand signals. The increased understanding you both experience will take your relationship to a deeper level. With more activities to enjoy together, your bond will stay fresh. A self-perpetuating process begins: The more you train, the stronger your bond. The better your bond, the more successful you'll be at training. If you think training is only the dictatorial imposition of your will upon your cat, you're forgetting the benefits she stands to enjoy.

If these gains sound too good to resist, keep in mind that every species has its problem child or two. Some cats will never do as you command, even if they love you more than a sunlit sofa. The timid cat has a hard time trusting the new requests. She may fear the props you use for training, such as hoops or jumps. The stubborn cat may love you but just choose not to listen to you. Not every cat was born to perform—but don't use this fact as an excuse not to try. The great majority of cats can learn many new tasks.

For the two hard cases above, try four weeks of fun, short training sessions. If the cat doesn't respond, accept the fact that she won't do your bidding. If you're still determined to teach your stubborn cat, you may want to work on some of the dominance exercises outlined in Chapter Two: Kitten Kindergarten. After you've shown her that you give the orders, she may just throw in the towel and comply.

Remember, too, that just as cats have preferences in the games they enjoy, they also fancy one type of trick more than another. It's best to pick an action your cat is naturally inclined to do. Some cats are better jumpers. Some cats prefer to sit and roll. Dr. Ribarich's cat Cookie prefers to work while stationary. Cookie's housemate Jake likes to move and be active. While picking which tricks to teach your cat, consider her activity level and unique personality.

Don't feel like a wimp if you and your cat naturally gravitate toward less demanding challenges like games. Training is probably the most intensive way we challenge our cats. There are many other activities and environmental modifications in this book to stimulate your cat's mind. Structured training isn't for everyone (or every cat).

Before You Start

Training cats takes an entirely different approach than does training dogs. We must tread a little more carefully to ensure the cat finds this process as entertaining and beneficial as we do. Basically, training is most successful when we shape some of the behaviors our cat already happily engages in. When teaching the cat any tricks, make sure to have the following factors in place.

1. *Strategy:* Some cat trainers encourage you to force your cat into position. While kittens are somewhat amenable to this treatment, many adult cats will dig their paws in and flatly refuse to comply. We have found that the most effective approach avoids pushing and pulling the cat into position. Instead, we recommend you manipulate her body by enticing her with a treat. Moving a food treat guides the cat's head, which in turn guides the rest of her body. If, despite all your efforts, you can't lead the cat into position with a treat, abandoning the exercise may be your only option.

2. *Training Area:* Start in an area where the cat feels comfortable. Keep the noise down—no television. Avoid distractions. It's wise to

choose a corner of the room so that her retreat would be a tad more difficult. Finally, training will be easier for both of you if your cat is on carpet.

3. *Schedule*: No Olympic regimen here. A mere three to five minutes once or twice a day, every day, until you feel she's gotten the hang of it will work best. Then move to once every other day to avoid her getting bored. Train just before dinner to ensure that she's properly motivated. A satiated cat may prefer to lounge rather than shake or roll over. Remember to keep to one trick at a time. Dr. Ribarich's cat learned her first trick, the sit, in two short training sessions. Everyone but the cat was surprised.

4. *Motivation:* Since cats aren't pack animals, simple praise or approval from the authority figure (owner) doesn't work as well as a tasty treat. If your cat doesn't have constant food available, her usual kibble may motivate her enough. Just make sure to train before a meal when she's most hungry. If you choose to use another kind of treat, it should remain special, used only when you're training. While it would be great to treat her to peanut butter or tuna, for her waistline and health, it's best to stick with canned wet food or tartar control kibble. A cat may develop vomiting or diarrhea if given certain foods, such as dairy products. Raw meat is never a good idea, as it can contain harmful bacteria or even parasites.

5. *Enforcement:* Each command must be met with an attempt at compliance from the cat. If the cat doesn't understand and doesn't move into the position, she doesn't get the treat. It's crucial that once you give the command, the cat assumes the position. Once she's in the position, reward. She must connect the proper position with the reward. Halfhearted attempts go unrewarded.

6. *Reward Schedule:* When the cat does respond correctly, make sure that you're giving the treat as closely as possible to the correct behavior. When first teaching, be fast and free with treats (of course giving them only when the cat is in the desired position). Cats need to know when they're doing right. Food tells them. Once the cat masters a trick, reward randomly. Keep the cat guessing as to when he'll get the treat. It's smart to make sure you reduce the amount of food at mealtime by the exact amount of treats you've bestowed upon the cat during training. It doesn't take much extra food to start putting on the padding. You want to avoid obesity at all costs.

In order to reward the correct behavior as closely as possible to its execution, you may want to try "clicker training." Popularized by trainer Karen Pryor and behaviorist Gary Wilkes, this training style involves using a small device that makes a clicking noise. The owner clicks the moment the animal has accomplished the task and then rewards with food as well. The click provides a secondary reinforcement to food. Clicker training works with cats, dogs, and many other types of animals. If you're interested in clicker training, Pryor's books and videos are available through Direct Book Service in Wenatchee, Washington (800–776–2665). Gary Wilkes maintains a website on the subject (www.clickandtreat.com). While some people swear by clicker training, remember that you can successfully train without this method.

7. *Commands and Hand Signals:* On top of your command word, develop some hand gestures to go along with the exercises you want to teach. Two types of commands, verbal and physical, convey our wishes more clearly. We'll describe possible hand gestures with every exercise.

8. *Owner Demeanor:* Don't confuse the cat with a lot of chatter. Avoid using "No" when the cat doesn't get into the proper position. Keep "NO" for when the cat is actively engaging in destructive behavior, such as climbing curtains. Using the cat's name even distracts the cat, so while you may want to use it at first to get her attention, don't overuse it.

9. *Release Word:* It's a good idea to have a word that signals to the cat that the exercise is over. An enthusiastic "all done" or "good kitty" works well. You may want to add a hand signal. Clasping your hands together is a common way to physically indicate that you're through making requests of the cat.

The First Trick: A Simple Sit

Teaching the first trick may be something of a shocker for the cat. She needs to get used to the fact that you're requesting behavior from her. Since she may struggle with this new concept, keep the actual exercise as simple as possible. Sit is a good one to start with because the cat sits a lot anyway, and you can praise her for doing what she does naturally. We wanted to start with sit because it is also a component of the more difficult tasks.

1. Pay attention when the cat is wandering about the room. Have your treats ready, but don't bother getting the cat's attention. The moment she sits, give her a treat and a "Good sit!" praise. Do that several times the first day, but don't go beyond the five-minute limit.

2. Felinesteins out there will pick up the sit without much further effort. Others may need a little help. If your cat hasn't connected your voice command with an action she is to perform, you'll need to be more direct. Put your cat in her training area. When she's standing, say "Sit." Holding a treat, lift your hand from in front of her nose to a point about six inches higher. This upward movement with the hand can be the sit hand signal. Then bring the treat up over the cat's head so that she's forced to sit as she watches the progress of the treat. The moment she sits, give her the treat. Say "Good sit!" and release. Repeat only two more times.

3. Once she sits well in her training area, get her to repeat the exercise in other places, even on top of tables. Animals learn in context, incorporating the environment into the exercise. To free her from this limitation, train in all areas once she performs the exercise well. Don't be surprised if she's completely clueless in the new area. You may have to backtrack and start over. She'll eventually be able to transfer her new skill to all areas.

Lie Down

Since you're still trying to get the cat accustomed to listening to you and responding, keep to simple exercises. Lie down is easily accomplished, but it may cause some trouble. Your cat may resist lying down because she feels more vulnerable in the prone position. If you persist and use treats, she'll see that there's something in it for her.

1. Put your cat in the usual training spot and get her to sit, either with your command and hand signal or by bringing the treat up over her head.
2. Once she's sitting, touch the cat's nose and then tap the ground, saying "Down." Tapping the ground will be your hand signal for lie down.
3. Hold the treat down on the floor under her nose. Pull the treat toward you five to six inches. The cat's inclination will be to lean for-

ward toward the treat. If you're lucky, she'll see that the best way for her to get the treat is to lie down. If you're unlucky, the cat will get up and walk toward the treat. Refuse to give the treat until the cat guesses the correct behavior. Yes, it *is* a guessing game. If the cat doesn't lie down, just end the training session. Try again the next day. If the cat gets up, repeat the sit command and try the steps above again. If you're still not getting anywhere, give up for that session and resume another time.

4. At first give the treat right away. In subsequent lie-down sessions, hold the treat for a few seconds so that the cat can't get it. Increase the time before you give the treat so the cat learns she must stay down for a little while. Praise and release.

Stay: The Useful Refrain

Because many games and training exercises require a stay, this feat will come in handy.

1. Make sure she understands sit first. Give her the sit command and maintain eye contact so that she's more likely to stay there. Sit four or five feet in front of her.

2. Reach toward her with the palm flat and open in an obvious stop motion. Say "Stay" once. If the cat tries to get up, guide her back into

the sit position with your treat. You may end up giving the sit command several times. Remember not to shout "No" if she rises. Simply get her back into the sit position using the treat.

3. Once she stays, wait only a couple of seconds. Reward with a treat and release.

4. Make her stay longer each time you ask until she stays for a count of ten.

5. To make things more challenging, start increasing the distance a bit between the two of you. Give the sit and stay command from a standing position.

Getting a Little Flashier: Roll Over

This trick impresses friends who think cats incapable of anything but sleep. Once again, you should start when the cat's already halfway there. When your cat is lying down with her feet in front before mealtime, have a treat on hand. Get your cat's attention. In the circus they do this by cracking a whip. We can do it by calling our cat's name.

1. Starting near the floor on one side of the cat's head, pass the treat in a circular motion over the cat's shoulders to the other side of her head. Say "Roll" as you do so. As her head turns to follow the treat,

her body will follow. Your hand signal becomes the slow circle you make in the air.

2. Once she has made a complete rotation, give her the treat and praise. Release. Eventually, you'll be able to teach the cat to lie down and then roll over.

A Circus Stand

Getting the cat to stand on her hind legs impresses people more than it should. Your audience won't know how easy it was to teach, so soak up their admiration with a smile.

Now are you happy?

1. Holding a treat, put the cat in a sit. Stand in front of her.

2. Hold the treat six inches over the cat's head. Make sure she realizes you have the treat, even if you have to bring it down to allow her to sniff it.

3. Snap the fingers of the treatless hand and say "Up" in a cheerful voice. The cat naturally tries to reach for the treat. She'll see her front two feet must leave the ground to win the reward.

4. Once the cat stays standing for a couple of seconds, give her the treat while she still holds that position.

The Old Rover Trick: Shake

And you thought only dogs could pull off this friendly greeting. Cats are happy to shake with you, although they may ask you to wash your hands first.

1. Put your cat in the usual training spot and get her to sit with your command and hand signal or by lifting the treat over the cat's head.
2. Extend your hand, palm upward, reaching toward her chest. This will be your hand signal for shake.
3. Say "Shake" and take her paw. While you still have her paw, give her the treat and praise. Release. Pretty quickly, the cat will raise her paw for you to take.

The Big Stunner: Bang, You're Dead

This amazing feat, modified from Mike Robertson's method, works best if you've exposed your cat to lots of Western movies. Actually, because cats like lying on their sides, getting them to do so on command isn't as difficult as it seems.

1. First wait around observing your cat. When she goes to lie down on her side, quickly jump in and say "Bang, you're dead." Reward her in that correct position. Repeat this for a week.

2. Now that she has an idea of what you want, when you get up in the morning, before you feed the cat, simply entice her with a piece of food held in your left hand. As you do so, hold the fingers on your right hand in a gun shape and say "Bang, you're dead." She'll look at you like you're nuts at first. Then she'll just stand there. But cats are no strangers to melodrama, and eventually she'll get your idea. Give your lie down command and hand signal. Once she's lying down, move your hand over to the right so that the cat must lie on her side to keep the treat in sight.

3. Once she's there on her side, reward her. It may take weeks, but eventually she'll go over on her side on your command. Simply incorporate the exercise into your morning routine. Get up, brush teeth, go downstairs, pull the treats from the fridge, say "Bang, you're dead" a couple of times, reward the cat if she responds and then get your breakfast. A little time and effort is returned with an impressive performance.

The Royalty Wave

This is a fun and easy one to teach.

1. Put your cat in the usual training spot and get her to sit either with your command and hand signal or by lifting the treat over her head.

2. Hold the treat high in the air within her line of sight and entice her with it. Wave the treat back and forth slowly in an arc that doesn't exceed nine inches or so. A limited back and forth motion in the air will be your hand signal for waving.

3. The cat will use her paw to bat at the treat. When she does, don't miss your chance to say "Wave."

4. Give the treat while she is waving. Praise and release. Repeat the exercise in other areas of the house.

...And to all my dedicated fans...

5. Eventually, she will wave simply with your hand signal and verbal command. Remember to reward constantly when first teaching a trick and then reward randomly. Once she performs consistently, give the treat every other time. Or reward twice

and then withhold rewards two times. Reward twice and then skip one. Keep the schedule varied.

Jumping

Since jumping comes quite naturally to cats, this trick will be fun for her.

1. Get a hurdle that's about ten to twelve inches high. A plank placed across a doorway works well. Secure the board against the door frame with cement blocks or bricks. Make sure it can't be knocked over. An unstable hurdle can spook a cat. Leave it in position for a week (if it doesn't endanger other family members). The cat will get used to its presence.

2. Put your cat on the other side of the barrier and have her sit and stay. If she won't perform a reliable sit, have someone hold her.

3. Tempt her over by holding up a special treat and calling her name.

4. Say "Jump," waving your hand in an arc in the air.

5. Praise, saying "Good jump!" as she is jumping. Give the treat as soon as you can after the jump.

6. Once she's jumping well, get her repeating the exercise in many areas of the house. Move the board to other doors and even let it stand freely in the middle of a room with the help of a couple more blocks or bricks.

Hula Hoop Jumping

This improvement on simple jumping makes people think you're really intelligent. For your own convenience, it's best to buy a small hula hoop. You can even use a bicycle tire. A four-foot length of garden hose, its ends joined with duct tape, works well, too. As you go through the exercise, try not to let the hoop wiggle too much or you'll spook the cat. You may need an assistant with this one.

1. Leave the hoop in her living area for a week, so she can sniff it and get used to it.

2. Kneel on the floor and hold the hoop between your knees so that it stands vertically.

3. Put the cat on the left of the hoop and hold her there by commanding, petting, or keeping a hand firmly on her back. With your right hand, pick up a treat.

4. Pass the treat through the hula hoop to your cat's nose, but don't allow her to take it. Let her stand and lead her through the hoop with the treat. Say "Jump" as she passes through. Notice that you say the command word while the animal is in the midst of performing the feat. Since you're using both hands just getting the cat through the hoop, forget the hand signal for now.

5. Once she's through the hoop, allow her to eat the treat. Praise and pet her.

6. Repeat this process until she's confidently stepping through the hoop. At this point you can even hold the hoop with one hand while she passes through. You won't need to restrain her.

7. Once she's passing through with confidence, raise the hoop one inch from the ground. You'll have to hold the hoop with your hand. Continue asking her to jump. Keep raising the hoop until she actually is jumping, but don't go above one foot from the floor. Keep enticing her with food. Remain sitting on your knees with all levels of this trick. It helps the cat feel secure.

8. Repeat in different areas of the house.

Scratching-Post Training: A Practicality

Too many cats get euthanized in the shelters because the owners didn't take the time to teach them to scratch appropriate objects. In the end, getting rid of the cat seems the least expensive, least frustrating route. If you understand a few facts about scratching preferences, scratching-post training becomes easy.

First, cats usually scratch at certain times: after waking from a nap and before and after eating. To direct these habits, place scratching posts near sleeping and eating areas. You should also observe your cat to determine when the itch to scratch is particularly strong for her. You may have to buy several, but a few scratching posts are less expensive than a parade of sofas. To make the scratching posts more enticing, they should be varied. Have one that is carpeted, another wound in sisal rope and even a cardboard version. Dr. Ribarich also highly recommends the Cat Scratch Feeder mentioned in Chapter Three: Home Alone. This scratching post rewards the cat by dispensing food as the cat pulls down on it.

Scratching posts are not limited to those you purchase in the store. One friend covered a cement post in her parking lot with sisal rope. Another wound rope around two rungs of her banister. Still another cat owner pasted a small piece of extra carpet to a rolling pin and hung it from a door knob. Scratching posts are relatively simple. You can make an inexpensive one yourself. Variety and accessibility are the keys to keeping the cat interested in her scratching post.

Scratching-post training works best when begun while your pet is still young. Below are the steps to creating a kitten that bypasses the sofa for the post every time.

1. With your kitten beside you, pretend to be the mother cat and scratch on the post yourself. We've already mentioned in Chapter Two: Kitten Kindergarten how the kitten learns best from the mother cat and the

owner she loves. The other benefit to scratching the post yourself is that it puts your scent on it, which will entice the cat to go there.

2. When the kitten actually scratches the post, praise her and reward with a treat. Positive reinforcements help animals learn much faster. Negative reinforcement (screaming at the kitten when she's scratching the ottoman) doesn't work as well on these little guys.

If you're hoping to train your adult cat to scratch at the post, you'll have to be consistent in using both positive and negative reinforcement. You have to make a good effort at taking the fun out of scratching inappropriate objects. Fill a soda can with pennies and throw it beside the cat when you catch her in the midst of this heinous behavior. Keep in mind to reward the correct behavior as much or even more than you discipline the incorrect one.

If you try these methods and the cat is still a determined couch-scratcher, you may want to try Soft Paws put out by SmartPractice. The first application of these plastic nail caps can be done at your veterinary clinic while you observe. You can take care of subsequent applications. For information, you can call SmartPractice at 800–433–7292. This alternative to declawing works for many owners. If you take the time to observe and guide your cat's scratching behavior, however, you'll probably be successful getting her to turn to the post.

Toilet Training Your Cat: Another Practical Trick to Make Your Life Easier

Sounds crazy, but it's not unheard of. Veterinarian Dr. Benjamin L. Hart, DVM, PhD, explains that teaching the cat to eliminate on the toilet takes little more from owners than gradually moving the location of the litter box. We've modified his suggestions below.

1. Put the litter box in the bathroom and wait until the cat is accustomed to eliminating in that room. It's best to put the litter box right next to the toilet.

2. Next, remove the toilet seat from the toilet. (This will be a tough trick for those with only one bathroom.) Shut the lid on the now rimless toilet. Securely attach the toilet seat to the top of the litter box. The cat learns to balance on the seat to eliminate.

3. Once you catch the cat balancing well, start increasing the height. If you have an adult cat, a stack of phone books added one at a time will work well. A kitten needs a much more gradual increase in height. Wait a few days between each new level.

4. Once the cat is eliminating with confidence at the normal height of the toilet, take the phone books away and securely fasten the litter box and seat to the toilet.

5. Your last step is to remove the litter box and put the toilet seat back where it started—with one modification. Affix a liner of clear, heavy plastic under the toilet seat. Poke a hole in the middle of the plastic and then put a layer of litter over it. The hole allows the urine to escape into the toilet.

6. Over the next ten days, gradually decrease the amount of litter. Once there is very little litter left, remove the plastic so that the cat is eliminating in the toilet with no props.

If you're looking for a shortcut, many pet supply stores sell kitty toilet training kits. The Kitty Whiz Transfer System available in most pet stores helps the cat make the leap from litter box to toilet bowl gradually. No matter what method you use, make sure this is the right thing for the cat. While it's fun to brag that your cat uses the toilet, if you find urine around your house, you'll know the cat just isn't a bowl kitty. Go back to the litter box and appreciate the muscles you build scooping.

Fluffy, the Supermodel

If your cat shocks the catnip out of you by embracing training, you may want to reveal her talent to the world. America's movie studios and corporations know how effectively cats capture the attention of the public. Producers look for cats on a regular basis. They know those in the 32 million American households that have cats love to see their furry friends on TV.

Before you dial an agent, however, make sure your cat can perform basic obedience commands (especially sit) as well as a few other tricks. Also, make sure your cat's personality fits with the Hollywood scene. The best cat actors have outgoing personalities and are not easily frightened. This cat welcomes visitors to your home and doesn't shrink away from new treasures retrieved from your latest shopping spree. In fact, the cat must be supercool. A lot of banging and crashing occurs on the set. As there probably won't be a bed for the cat to run and hide under, you'll be chasing her through all sorts of props. The sight of your frantically fleeing backside won't impress directors.

If you think your cat could be the next Morris, your first step will be to get some professional photographs taken. Take a full body shot, a head shot and a shot where the cat is doing or wearing something unusual. Professional photographers can best reflect what your cat has to offer. Since many photographers specialize in pets, look until you find an experienced one. You can dress the cat. In fact, since some commercials now require the cat to wear something, having a photo of your cat in clothing may prove a plus.

The next step is to look up "Animal Rental," "Animal Brokers," or "Talent Agencies" in the yellow pages to find agencies that handle cats. Beware of agencies that charge up-front fees. Their only fees should be in the form of the commission they receive from your pet's work. This rate runs from between 10 and 25 percent. Ask whether the agency is licensed with the

United States Department of Agriculture. That the agency was screened by the USDA will ease your mind. Send each appropriate agency a description of your cat, how long you've been training her, and the basic obedience exercises and tricks she can perform. You also want to include vitals such as her weight, height, breed, and age.

Sometimes, if the talent agencies like the look of your cat, they'll go to the trouble of training her for specific exercises. In fact, there's usually a cat trainer on staff. Nevertheless, the most impressive cat already performs a number of charming tricks. Most agencies like to see that you and your cat have been training for a while.

Be prepared—casting agents do not focus solely on the cat. They're looking at the neurosis level of the owner as well. Agents don't want the producers they work with to suffer from stage parents ready to burst on the set screaming about their cat's makeup. When you meet with the agent, convey your confidence in the integrity of the agency and the producers with whom they contract.

Actually, owners don't need to be too worried about the well-being of their up-and-coming star on the set. On every production, the law requires that a representative from the American Humane Association is present to make sure that all animals are well-rested, exercised, fed, and watered. Also, on every show, a trainer oversees the animals. Ever since a stuntman rode a horse off a 70-foot cliff during the filming of *Jesse James* in 1939, producers and directors have been cautious about caring for all animals involved.

Despite a film crew's best intentions, however, sometimes owners who stay on the set find their cats' needs being overlooked. Amidst the frantic pace of a take, cats have been left in hot sun for longer than owners like. Cats have been lost when escaping from unlatched crates between takes. If you feel your cat is not getting the treatment you had expected and your complaints are being ignored, be prepared to walk off the set with the cat. While most Hollywood cats receive star pampering, you want to be on hand to make sure your cat receives this treatment. Filming is a long, boring day, so you'll be sacrificing a good chunk of time. Keep these negatives in mind when considering a stage career for your cat.

Know, too, that financial independence won't come to you through your kitty's good looks. Payment for a day on the set is about $450. Without unions, cats haven't been able to win residuals. If you get a commercial, expect to receive about $125 per hour. These fees seem reasonable, but after the agency siphons off their portion and can get you only one gig per year, you've got to be in it for love.

In Short. . .

Your cat may seize upon the American work ethic and toil diligently for you. Paul Loeb, coauthor of *You Can Train Your Cat*, has trained hundred of cats for movies and television commercials. He claims that some cats are natural workers and natural actors. Your cat may be one of them. While training, make sure the cat's treats plus her meals add up to a healthy diet. By reducing the amount of food you give at mealtime according to how many treats you handed out, you'll prevent your cat from snagging an extra meal from you each day. If you're going to train, remember that the tricks she learns won't necessarily make your life easier. She'll never diaper children or vacuum. If you're lucky, you'll get her to wave a paw, roll over, or sit. Why bother then? Your effort comes back to you in the form of the intellectual, physical, and emotional benefits your cat will enjoy. The challenge you bring to your cat's life should be your focus, not any gains you stand to make with a trick-trained cat.

6

The Intellectual Fat Cat

SHAPING THE BODY, TONING THE MIND

I'm not fat, I'm Fluffy!

Cats are careful to maintain their dignity...that is, until the creamy French vanilla emerges from the refrigerator. Then, all nobility crumbles. They twine around our legs begging: "Oh please! Ice cream for me!" And when a little ice cream brings so much happiness, we're glad to oblige.

You're not surprised then that a 1992 study reported in the *Journal of Small Animal Practice* found that 40 percent of pet cats were either overweight or obese. Researchers point to two culprits: decreased daily activity of indoor cats and increased availability of "highly palatable" cat foods. As mentioned before, the number of strictly indoor cats now approaches that of cats with access to the outdoors. With all the trees and fences there, outdoor cats just get to move more. As numbers of indoor cats rise, so too will the client list of veterinarians treating weight and behavior problems.

The other culprit, "highly palatable foods," shows us how well consumers have responded to commercials promoting high-fat, rich-tasting meals. When these feasts appear on television as puffs of chocolate mousse resting in crystal goblets, who can resist? The fat riddled throughout dinners like these sends "palatability" off the scale. Although we'd like to think of our cats as reserved, they will keep stuffing their faces after they're full. In fact, researchers found that a cat will eat more of the high-fat meals regardless of whether he's really hungry or not (sound familiar?). While we carefully select wheat germ and tofu for ourselves, we stagger toward the high-fat cat foods like zombies. And nary a cat is complaining.

While we want to give our cats the best and protect them from all dangers, superpremium foods combined with supersedentary lifestyles erode our pets' health. Obese cats are at a much higher risk for heart and liver disease. A fit heart would have a hard enough time carrying around the extra pounds the obese cat stockpiles. Overweight cats are also at greater risk for respiratory difficulty, diabetes, and arthritis. If the cat manages to skirt these frightening disorders, there's solid evidence that obesity accelerates the aging process. Clearly, if you want to get your cat to the far end of the age range, keep him fit.

But everyone knows excess weight impacts health whether you're a cat, a person or a rhinoceros. What place does obesity have in a book about cat intelligence? Plenty. There's solid evidence that physical health has a profound effect on brainpower. Dr. Marilyn Albert, associate professor of psychology and neurology at Harvard and director of gerontology at Massachusetts General Hospital, studied one thousand people from age seventy to eighty. She found that those who had engaged in strenuous activity throughout their lives maintained their cognitive skills far better than sedentary participants. Apparently, increased blood flow to the brain—arriving courtesy of a vigorous circulatory system—helps the brain perform at peak levels. Albert also found that healthy lung function contributed to brain fitness. Lungs working at maximum capacity create the most oxygen-rich blood, a cocktail on which the brain thrives. These tests, while conducted on humans, demonstrate how healthy respiratory and circulatory systems reinforce any mammalian brain.

The bottom line is that a healthy cat probably thinks better than a fat one. The above scientific evidence simply reinforces what we all come to from our own commonsense observations: A fit cat has more ability and opportunity to put himself into learning situations. Engaging in games, exploring the house and yard, and even taking some walks remains beyond the abilities of the obese cat. A cat who can participate in these activities energizes both body and brain.

Just as fitness and mental engagement support each other, weight gain and boredom fuel each other on a downward spiral. Obesity is one of the sure signs of severe boredom. The veterinarian with an overweight cat on his or her examining table often asks how active the cat is, how much time he spends playing, and what type of activities he enjoys, on top of diet-related questions. The doctor is fishing for how much stimulation the cat gets. Why? Most overweight cats have little access to stimulation. In fact, for the bored cat, food serves as one of the few ways to stimulate the senses. Research studies have shown that completely sedentary animals actually consume more food and gain more weight than do moderately active animals. If the sedentary animal's only activity is the long walk to the food bowl, it's no wonder he makes the trip several times. Your cat's excess weight could be a signal to you that he needs more interaction and fun. Often, cats crave more than nourishment when they eat.

Addressing the boredom is an important step in treating the obesity. Before you reach for the kitty dumbbells, however, first determine whether your cat ranks with the technically obese. The medical definition of obesity is 15 to 20 percent over ideal weight. Some cats, like people, have a high enough metabolism to burn an avalanche of calories. If that seems to be the case with your cat, stick to a schedule of games and environmental modifications recommended in Chapter Three: Home Alone and Chapter Four: Games and Toys to Keep the Mind Purring. If you're unsure whether your cat presses the scales to the breaking point, these clues will help you make that determination.

Fat-Cat Indicators

You know your cat is overweight when. . .

1. You can't remember when you last saw his neck. There's just a nose and two eyes centered between his shoulder blades.
2. He can no longer get his entire head in the cookie jar.
3. When your cat jumps onto the bed, it crashes to the floor.
4. The floorboards under his litter box squeak.

Actually, it's easy to determine whether your cat is at a healthy weight. You should just be able to feel the outline of each of his ribs. As you stroke him from his shoulder to his hip, the fit cat's side curves inward, resulting in a tapered waist. You should be able to see this curve starting at the end of the ribs, just by looking down at the cat's back while he's standing. If while petting your cat's side, you can't locate a waist (perhaps you locate a basketball instead), take him to a veterinarian for a thorough physical exam. The veterinarian will determine your cat's current weight and his ideal weight and then suggest a diet and exercise strategy.

If your cat is overweight, don't cut back too drastically right away. A rapid loss of weight can result in serious liver problems. Veterinarians have found that a loss of one percent of body weight per week is the most healthy and sustainable level. With these goals, an eight-pound cat loses about 1.5 ounces per week. Realistically, it takes eight to twelve months to reach ideal weight.

After the weight melts away, cats struggle to keep it off, just like humans do. The biggest reason for failure in the feline world is not dieter weakness. Veterinarians find time after time that it's the owner who has not complied with the diet. In other words: Kitty's too cute; Mommy caved in to begging.

When Food Is More Than Sustenance

Food means a lot to many species, including ours. It forges the bonds between the members of human families, starting with the crucial infant-mother bond established through breast- or bottle-feeding. Later, both mother and father provide and prepare the meals that unite and organize family life. Even grandmothers contribute to the feeding frenzy. When the third helping of mashed potatoes drops from Grandma's serving spoon to your plate, she vibrates with joy. Food carries and sends many emotional messages.

Food conveys messages between species as well. For cat owners, giving our cats several meals and a few snacks daily feels much more loving than doling out a mere two servings of dry kibble. Why else did we get our cats but to feel more love in our lives? We sense what scientists have finally documented: The act of providing food helps establish and sustain the bond between pet and owner. Because of the feeding process, the cat learns to depend upon the owner for its well-being. The owner appreciates the cat's trust and enjoys the responsibility. But we can further the bonding process in other ways. Recognizing the emotional benefits we receive from feeding can help us prevent unhealthy overfeeding.

Why are we focusing on the owner's mushiness when it's the cat that gets fat? The biggest reason cats can't lose weight lies not in metabolism, appetite, or genetics, but *you*, the owner. You control the food. This control is usually a good thing—unless the cat controls you. Cats put on a lot of weight between meals when they "help" us prepare dinner or clean our plates. Owners that cannot resist a plaintive cry or gentle paw on the hand as they handle food end up with heavy cats. Further complicating things, the variety present in our scraps or leftovers entices cats to eat past their natural satiation point. It's no wonder they beg.

Where the treating owner caves in to begging, the overfeeding owner can't seem to stop himself from pouring a Mt. Everest of cat food into the bowl. Because some cats do overeat, it's not wise to leave a constant supply of food available. Stick to the guidelines set by your veterinarian.

Curbing Your Feeding Behavior

Despite all the sound logic behind feeding a cat reasonably, many can't stop themselves from treating and overfeeding. Because cat owners are reluctant to abandon this pampering, we've included gentle ways to modify the delivery of meals and snacks.

First, note the most common times your cat begs and the amount he usually wins from you. The next time he begs, reduce the amount you give him. Over the following week, keep reducing it until it's eliminated or at least significantly less. If the cat's begging becomes even more aggressive as you decrease, you'll have to put him in another room. Since he probably doesn't want to separate from you at this time, he'll learn he needs to quiet down. Another strategy is to keep some healthy, maybe even less flavorful, snacks on hand for those times when he's set on begging. You can substitute vegetables for the chicken fat or milk you used to slip him. Some cats like vegetables. In fact, the grass and houseplants they maul show just how much they can enjoy their greens. Coauthor Suzanne Delzio had one cat that found rose petals irresistible, making it difficult for her husband to ever bring home flowers (jewelry proved a good substitute). To discover which veggies your cat enjoys, experiment. Your cat may have a favorite that you can use regularly as a healthy treat or even a dinner supplement.

Treating's happy brother, overfeeding, blows our cats up like puffer fish. We could advise you to cut down on the amount of food you feed, but that would be too logical. Admit it, you're too weak. Because cats do enjoy eating, one way to give him the amount he craves is to simply buy a low-calorie, high-fiber cat food. Fiber is recommended by some animal nutritionists because it is poorly digestible and dilutes the digestion of fats and calories in a diet. Animals can consume a greater volume of the high-fiber diet without consuming more calories. Further, a high-fiber diet may help the cat feel fuller faster. Since some "light" products contain more calories than others, read the labels carefully. Prescription weight-reduction diets, either of the high-fiber or low-fat variety, are also available from veterinary clinics. Because we hate to skimp, the regular amount of a light food gives the cat the pleasure of eating while siphoning off a few calories.

A better strategy for addressing snacking and overfeeding circumvents food altogether. Veterinary behaviorist Dr. Bonnie Beaver and Psychology professor Dr. Margaret Norris, writing in *The Journal of the American Veterinary Medical Association,* suggest that owners replace feeding with other forms of bonding. In doing so, we can find the strength to feed the leftovers to the disposal. Grooming, playing, talking, and training all reinforce your relationship with your cat and can be successful substitutes for feeding. At first, these activities may not seem to pack the love punch that food does, but rest assured that they are just as bonding. Norris and Beaver recommend that, when your cat begs, try to get him interested in a game. Have some toys available in the kitchen or eating area. A game will distract him from his goal of getting food from you. Another way to redirect his attention is to have a comb ready and groom him. Intent on a snack, he may resist these diversions at first, but most cats happily give in to grooming or playing when you're persistent.

Since we, the authors, believe in the benefits of training your cat, we'd like to extend the above suggestion to include working on your cat's tricks. The next time he begs, ask for a sit or a paw wave. Here again, you're substituting one form of bonding with another. Don't think you're cheating.

When working on an exercise with your cat, you not only talk to him, but you probably touch him as well. In fact, you're interacting with him even more than if you were simply to throw him a bit of tuna casserole. On the whole, if you train, play with, and groom your cat regularly, you won't cave as easily to his whining. You'll be confident you give your cat the best care. With lots of attention going both ways, no one feels deprived.

Again targeting you, the overfeeder/treater, Norris and Beaver recommend another way to change your behavior. Set up a new household rule: The cat will eat only from his bowl. All food and snacks must start there. He'll learn this new rule quickly, but his part of the bargain isn't as crucial as yours. If you're relaxing on the couch or bed with a bowl of goodies and the cat starts to beg, you'll have to get up and move. The thought of that extra energy you'd have to expend may just strengthen your resolve to hold out against a begging cat at your elbow. This trick works best with owners competent at self-discipline. When executed consistently, the cat learns that when he's outside of his eating area, he won't be eating. The begging dies down. . . if you're strong!

Kitty's Part of the Weight-Reducing Bargain

There are two ways to slim down any mammal: Reduce the input or increase the output. If you can curb your feeding behavior, you have half the fat conquered. Those who have studied obesity in companion animals explain that, although some can be predisposed genetically to obesity, most cases are a result of overfeeding, under-exercising, or a combination of the two. If you control the feeding, you can leave exercising to the cat. Simply set up the conditions and equipment so that he can exercise, and you're on your way.

The heavy cat needs a slow entry into the world of exercise. With a few modifications to the environmental suggestions in Chapter Three: Home Alone, your cat can have his own kitty gym. While you may be enthusiastic about getting into a program to help your cat become healthier, there are special precautions and modifications to make when stimulating the overweight cat.

Exercise Equipment

The multilevel climbing towers and ten-foot scaling net suggested in Chapter Three: Home Alone may be a bit beyond your cat's capabilities at this point. Now matter how big their bellies get, cats' legs seem to stay slim.

Those little legs can only heft so much poundage. Start with the ramps or kitty staircases affixed to the wall. Keep climbing posts low.

The best exercise equipment for a heavy cat is a playful companion. The cat will have more incentive to play and he can do so at his own pace. As he loses weight, his playing vigor will increase. Once again, take the precautions in Chapter Three: Home Alone before bringing a new cat into your home.

In Chapter Three: Home Alone, we described the kitty treasure hunt where your cat watches you as you place treats in partially hidden areas around the house. This game keeps the cat moving from room to room, burning calories and sparking curiosity. To modify it for the big boy or girl, start by replacing treats with his favorite vegetable, a few high-fiber kibbles, or even catnip toys. Don't use too many and try to place them as far apart as possible to get the cat walking decent distances. Remember to let him watch you when you plant the treats. You may even want to put the treats on small paper plates so that he can see them more easily.

If, however, you want to avoid putting a big brussels sprout on your carpeting, cat perches at the opposite ends of the cat's living area also get the cat moving. Make sure the two windows you choose offer exciting vistas and are as far away from each other as possible. Two perches keep your cat going back and forth, particularly if you have east- and west-facing windows so that the cat can get the morning sun and then shift locations to soak up those afternoon rays.

It's not only a multiplicity of perches that can entice your heavy cat. If he responds well to one television, consider setting up an appliance timer on the bedroom television, if you're fortunate enough to have two. If you set up appliance timers on both televisions, you can have an animal-oriented program playing from 11:00 to 11:05 in the bedroom. After the excitement, the kitty is just getting some rest when the living room television bursts into bird song at 1:00. You can have the kitty going back and forth all day. If there's a set of stairs in between, so much the better.

Games for Hefty

The Slim Faster Version of the Hide-and-Seek Game: An enticing, more mellow version of hide-and-seek described in Chapter Four: Games and Toys to Keep the Mind Purring works well with the food-motivated cat. Simply get a few low-calorie treats or vegetable pieces. It's wise to take them from the cat's mealtime ration. Before dinnertime, when he's hungry, call him to you. Put two of the treats down at your feet. While he's busy eating the treats, walk a few feet away and wait for your cat to look up at you or call him. Let him see you putting two more treats at your feet. He will move to you again. This time move around the corner. Keep increasing the distance until you are moving from room to room. This game will get the cat walking. Try to sustain it for at least ten minutes.

When playing any kind of game, don't let the cat slack. His weight will make it easier for him to slip into laziness. If you play with him with a feather toy, make sure he's on his feet much of the time. Don't let him get away with lying on his back swatting the feather with two front paws like a giant beached walrus. Try to keep him on his feet and moving for ten or more minutes in any game.

While these walking and playing strategies burn calories, toys can also aid you in the fight against fat. Start a new habit with new toys. Each time you buy a toy (or adapt a piece of safe garbage), let your cat see it, but quickly toss it for a game of fetch or hide it under a barrier (letting him see you do so). Walk across the room and put it on the back of the couch where he will have to climb for it. Ask for a little effort for every fun thing you do for him. If he doesn't move for the thrown toys, reduce the distance to find the point at which he will expend some energy. Then gradually throw the toy farther and farther. You'll both get into the habit of movement.

As far as toys go, heavy cats respond well to the Play-N-Treat described in Chapter Four: Games and Toys to Keep the Mind Purring. (Of course they do—there's food in it!) You can also use the homemade version of this ingenious toy: your toilet paper roll containing the kibble that falls from the holes cut into it. The cat that loves food cannot resist pawing these toys around in hopes of freeing a morsel. Remember to subtract the amount of food you put in these contraptions from the cat's usual ration to avoid overfeeding.

To give his mind some satisfaction he can draw upon in those long hours apart from you, train him. Boredom—the initiator of obesity—accumulates.

If he had a challenging evening with you, he may not be so bored the whole next day. His brain will have been satisfied. Excited by the training you did together, he'll have more of a reason to move his body around. If you're stimulating him with challenges, he won't be as driven to stimulate his senses by eating. Of course, you wouldn't start your feline tanker out on hoop jumping. Waving may be just the trick he'd enjoy. In training, use your low-calorie treats or vegetables. Here's an important training trick for the heavy cat: A tiny food reward motivates as well as a large one. The cat doesn't need half a hot dog to know he has done well. A morsel you can barely keep between two fingertips is big enough. Once again, it's smart to engage in these activities before dinner when the cat is hungry.

In Short. . .

Getting your cat's weight under control can be a fun project for both of you. It doesn't require Nautilus machines, crystals, and incense—or pineapple-only diets. A little more walking, a tad less eating, and you're on your way. Understanding why you are prone to overfeeding your cat helps you stop your unhealthy habits. Substitute food with play, grooming, and training. Remember that the heart and lungs of a lean, healthy cat pumps more oxygen-rich blood to his hungry brain. While Kitty may pout when denied that luscious glob of chicken fat, he'll feel and think much better in the long run.

7

The Wise Elder

". . . I see cats that are 'old' at nine years of age and others that are 'young' at fifteen. The environment in which the cat finds itself can speed up or slow down its genetically predetermined life span. This is the area that we can influence by providing a stimulating environment, one that keeps the brain active."

BRUCE FOGLE, DVM, in *The Cat's Mind*

When looking at our elderly cats, we suddenly go soft. We lower our voices and tread a little lighter. We keep them away from loud noises and maybe even slip them a little of that high-fat cat food we've been careful to avoid all these years. Cats melt into our pampering arms like butter into a potato. "More indulgence?" they think. "For me? Well, if saying 'no' would hurt your feelings. . . "

We may enjoy doling out the extra loving, but we should be careful about our perceptions of our older, shorter housemates. The more we regard them as geriatric and infirm, the more cautious we are of challenging them. Cats need an invigorating life far into their golden years.

As the above quote from *The Cat's Mind* reflects, brain researchers no longer accept that mental decline must accompany aging. Formerly, the theory went that brain cells inevitably died off as the years ticked by. People held this to be just as true for those who kept mentally busy as for those who did not. No one was immune from age's relentless advance.

New findings have turned that idea on its head. Now, researchers attribute much of the loss of brainpower to lack of challenge in a lifetime. If the brain isn't used, it gets lazier and lazier. Of course, after decades of ennui, its lowest point is found in old age. While there have been no studies done on intellectual competence and aging in cats, we can adapt some important lessons from those involving people.

The Seattle Longitudinal Study provides some of the best evidence of the "use it or lose it" theory of brain growth and maintenance. Still continuing today, the study's duration and number of participants makes it one of the most credible examples in brain research. Since its inception in 1956, researchers have been tracking more than five thousand people aged twenty to ninety. In it, Dr. K. Warner Schaie, who is now director of the Gerontology Center at Penn State University, examined what happens to intellectual abilities as people age. Results from the last forty years indicate that the sharpest elders of the lot not only had a high level of education but continued to challenge their minds with satisfying work, reading, travel, culture, classes, clubs, and professional organizations. These folks all shared a sense that their lives made a difference and their work was meaningful. A vocation or hobbies with challenge and purpose kept their minds in top shape.

When Schaie and his colleagues turned to those participants who weren't engaged in the above activities, the results were just as revealing. The less active, underchallenged participants actually lost brainpower over the years. The brain drain and ensuing lack of confidence became a vicious cycle. The less these participants challenged themselves, the faster they lost skills and quickness. With new activities or vocations more difficult to master, they were less motivated to try them. This study concluded that lifestyle choices impacted the longevity of intelligence as much as, if not more than, any physical loss set in motion by a ruthless genetic code.

Even though this study was done on humans, we can apply some of its findings to our aging cats. We've already discussed at length how the results from studies based on one species translated effectively to others. By cleverly adapting the methods used by alert seniors of our own species, we can help keep our elderly cats mentally spry.

Before we suggest how to rev the older cat's engine, though, it's wise to consider the physical differences between a senior cat and her daughter. While the deceleration of a cat's mental abilities hinge on her lifestyle, there's no denying that the older cat does slow down physically. We need to be aware of limitations when seeking out challenges for her.

Technically, a cat is considered geriatric after age ten (75 percent of her expected life span). While the average feline life span runs to twelve to fifteen years, there are quite a few twenty-year-old cats still making their way to the window perch. All five senses of the older cat do diminish to some extent. With the cat's metabolism slowing down sometimes by as much as 30 percent, she may need less food. The number and size of muscle cells decrease, and arthritis becomes common. Cardiac output also decreases by as much as 30 percent between midlife and old age. These physical changes slow the cat down and entice her to sleep more often.

It's not only the cat's physique that's affected. Cognitive dysfunction can also occur in old age. An older cat who begins to eliminate in the wrong place or yowl at night may be experiencing a feline version of "senility." Having a thorough physical examination by your veterinarian twice a year will catch problems early, saving you money and your cat needless suffering.

Despite these limitations, the Cornell Feline Health Center and many other animal organizations stress that your cat's final years can and should be filled with "moderate activity." Games, walks and interesting things to explore all fill the bill. The increased oxygen in the blood (due to exercise) carried to the brain will enrich it, keeping it as sharp as possible. Beyond the intellectual benefits, regular and sustained bouts of play and movement help maintain muscle tone, enhance circulation, improve digestion, and prevent excess weight gain in our elderly cats. In determining the level of "moderate activity" she prefers to engage in, let your cat take the lead.

While you may have to start the fun, it's best to let the elderly cat decide when to end it. A cat lets you know she has had enough when she lies down and seems disinterested or bluntly walks away. Cat owners have nothing to fear from a good dose of moderate activity.

While it's admirable to spur your geriatric cat to intellectual heights, you want to be more careful with Grandma than with a resilient kitten—and not just because of health concerns. Of all the types of cats, geriatric pets resist changes in daily routine the most. Household moves, the introduction of a new pet, or a change in the owner's work schedule might bring on a bout of depression or instigate destructive behavior. Introducing changes gradually and allowing the elderly pet sufficient time to adapt can minimize stress and stave off behavior problems. For instance, if you want to add some of the cat furniture recommended in Chapter Three: Home Alone, start with one object (preferably the smallest) at a time. Leave anything you plan to affix to the wall or window on the floor for a week, so the cat can examine it safely. Introduce one game at a time, and stick with it for a month or so. After the cat has mastered it, then move on to the next one. While you want to keep your cat on her cerebral toes, keep in mind her greatest limiting factor: She has become set in her ways, used to a routine that may not even be good for her. It's up to you to lead her into a more exciting daily life. . . slowly.

The elderly cat, too, may not respond well to the best exercise and exploratory device: a cat companion. Adding another to the very established household may distress the older cat. In some cases, a new cat may reanimate an older cat. The chances are greater, however, that the new addition will simply tick her off. This stress of the presence of a new cat can be eased if you give the older cat more affection and attention for the first few weeks after you bring the new cat home.

Keeping Our Elderly Cats Sharp Day to Day

If humans retain their intellectual skills by engaging in interesting work and education, how can cats do the same if they have no access to challenging jobs or even an extended university? Simple. Education and invigorating work is the exploration and mastery of new concepts. We can provide that for our cats by devising new games for them, providing new places to explore, and helping them learn new skills.

Chapter Three: Home Alone, Chapter Four: Games and Toys to Keep the Mind Purring, and Chapter Five: Trick Training to Increase Brainpower give specific examples of ways to keep our cats moving and thinking. Sedate

A little catnip puts the scratch back into the old claws!

versions of each activity work for the older cat. If your cat lives to fifteen, however, you have a lot of years to fill with games and tricks. Even if your cat is just entering her golden years now, you still could have five or more years to entertain her. You'll run through the activities here in a couple of years. Then what?

Keeping the right attitude helps you happily maintain your long-term commitment to your cat's inner life. The purpose of engaging the cat in games and trick training is not to create a cat that can entertain audiences. Rather, the purpose of training and gaming is to give the cat a daily dose of challenge—ten minutes each day will suffice. Many people are put off by training because they fear they won't get results fast enough. They dread their own and their cat's failure. These folks need to shift their focus from themselves to the cat. Getting the cat to do a lot of tricks feeds your ego. On the other hand, providing your cat with some fun and adventure puts her needs first. Professional trainers consider training to be a lifelong process. All the better for us. If you lower your expectations, knowing that it may take you a month to teach your cat the paw wave, you will stick with it more dependably. Value the process over the product; the process is much longer and more important anyway.

One way to expand your options with the elderly cat requires no extra effort. It depends on a little-known fact: Animals learn in context of the environment. Dolphin trainers often lament that while a dolphin may have mastered a task in one tank, she has no idea how to perform it in another. In the confines of the new tank, the trainer has to start over from the beginning. Trainers groan about the same rigidity in horses, cats, and dogs. While it may be an irritation for trainers, it helps us keep the cat's mind working.

A new environment in which to play a familiar game could make the game itself seem new. In the changed surroundings, the cat has new obstacles to watch out for and new colors and shapes to take in as she learns. This shortcut keeps old games fresh. Once you change where you usually play or train, don't be surprised if you have to start training from the beginning again. It's not tedious. Your discouragement is inappropriate. Keep in mind that you are providing your cat with her ten minutes of daily challenge. You're not trying to start your circus with her. If she does need retraining, so much the better for you. You've given her a way to practice her skills. You're a good owner.

In Short. . .

When addressing elderly cats, the focus usually rests upon making them comfortable. Perhaps we should make them a bit uncomfortable. We can keep them mentally stretching until they reach the end. Welsh poet Dylan Thomas in his poignant plea to his dying father wrote, "Do not go gentle into that good night. Rage, rage at the dying of the light." Just because your cat is moving a little more slowly doesn't mean she must while away her days in sleep. Revitalize your old cat with games, tricks, and a thrilling environment. Don't be content to simply let her slip quietly into old age, having reassured yourself that you've met all her food and shelter requirements. This gal still needs the spice that makes life worth living.

Whether your cat is young or old, filling her days with challenge, variety, novelty, physical exercise, interesting things to see, and quality time with you ensures that her life means something. While this book has more than a hundred suggestions, simply making a few environmental changes, learning a new game every once in a while, and teaching her a trick or two will do wonders in giving your cat a rich existence. Your cat gives you a great deal: love, security, purpose, and connectedness, among other gifts. In return she asks for a little food and a lot of attention. You can spice up the attention you bestow with training, walking, playing, and watching together. A little of your time blooms into a lot of pleasure and contentment for you both. Remember, who scores the highest on the intelligence test is not the crucial issue. It's who is making the best use of what intelligence they have. Find any creature, human or feline, using its brain to its potential and you have found a content and happy soul.